THERE IS NOTHING LEFT TO LOSE

CONTENTS

Music transcriptions by Pete Billmann, Colin Higgins, Jeff Perrin, and Jeff Jacobson

ISBN 0-634-01320-3

Photography by Danny Clinch

Photography by Danny Clinch

Photography by Danny Clinch

Stacked Actors

Words and Music by Dave Grohl, Nate Mendel and Taylor Hawkins

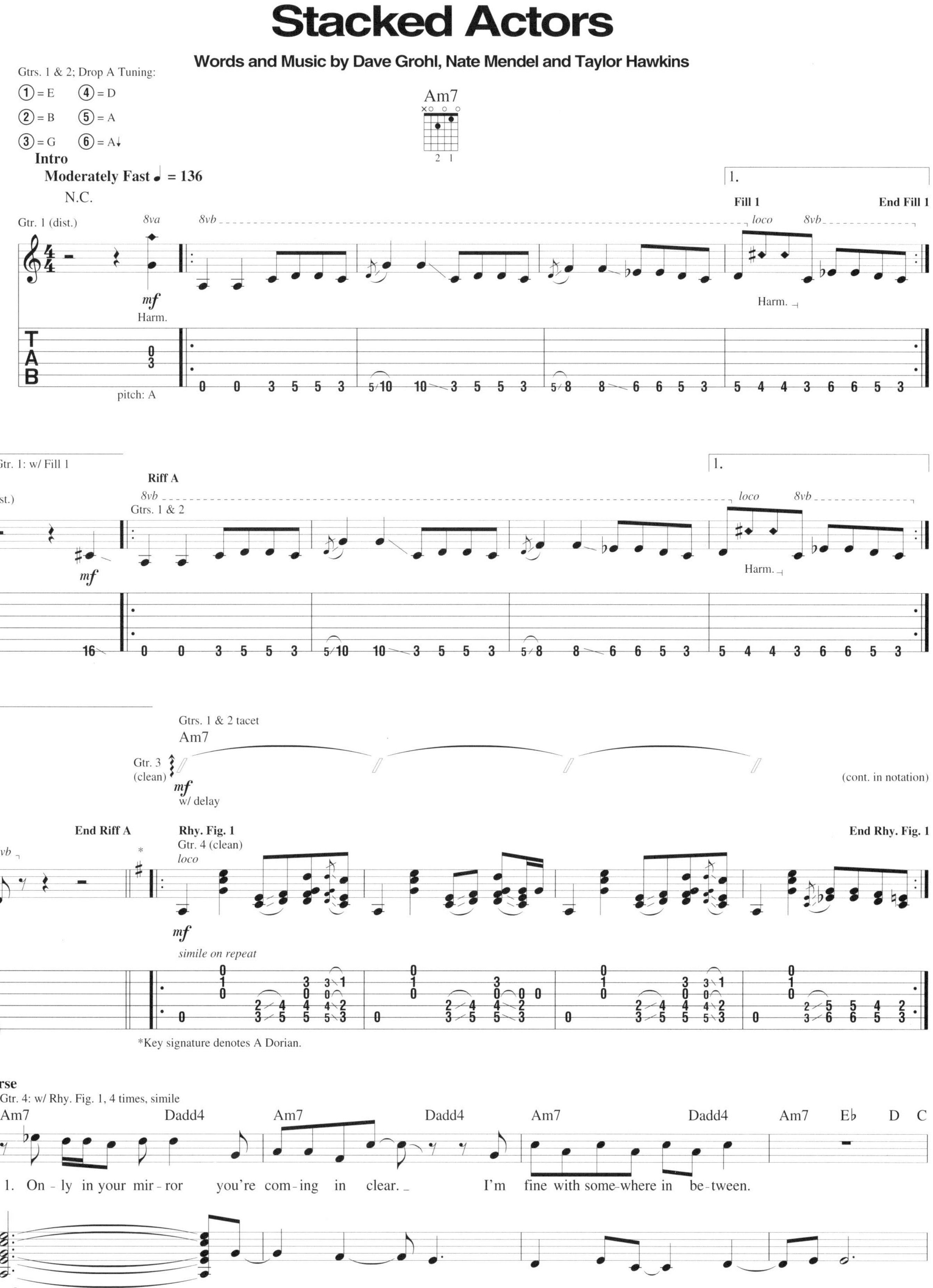

Gtr. 4: w/ Rhy. Fig. 1, 3 times, 2nd time, simile
Am7 Dadd4 Am7 Dadd4 Am7 Dadd4 Am7 E♭ D C
I'm im - pressed, what a beau - ti - ful chest. I nev - er meant to make a big scene.
2. God bless, what a sen - si - tive mess, yeah but things aren't al - ways what they seem.
simile on repeat
Will you re - sign to the lat - est de - sign? You look so mes - sy when you dress up in dreams.
Your tear - y eyes, your fa mous dis - guise, nev - er know - ing who to be - lieve.
One more for hire or won - der - ful li - ar? I think it's time we all should come clean.
See through, yeah, but what do you do when you're just an - oth - er an - cient drag queen?
Harm.
8va
Gtrs. 1 & 2
Gtr. 3
divisi
pitch: A
Pre-Chorus
Gtr. 4: w/ Rhy. Fig. 1, simile
Am7 Dadd4 Am7 Dadd4 Am7 Dadd4 *Am7 E♭/A D/A C/A
Stacked dead ac - tors, stacked to the raft - ers. Line up the bas - tards, all I want is the truth. Hey, hey,
Gtr. 3
8vb
Gtrs. 1 & 2
loco
*Chord symbols reflect combined tonality.

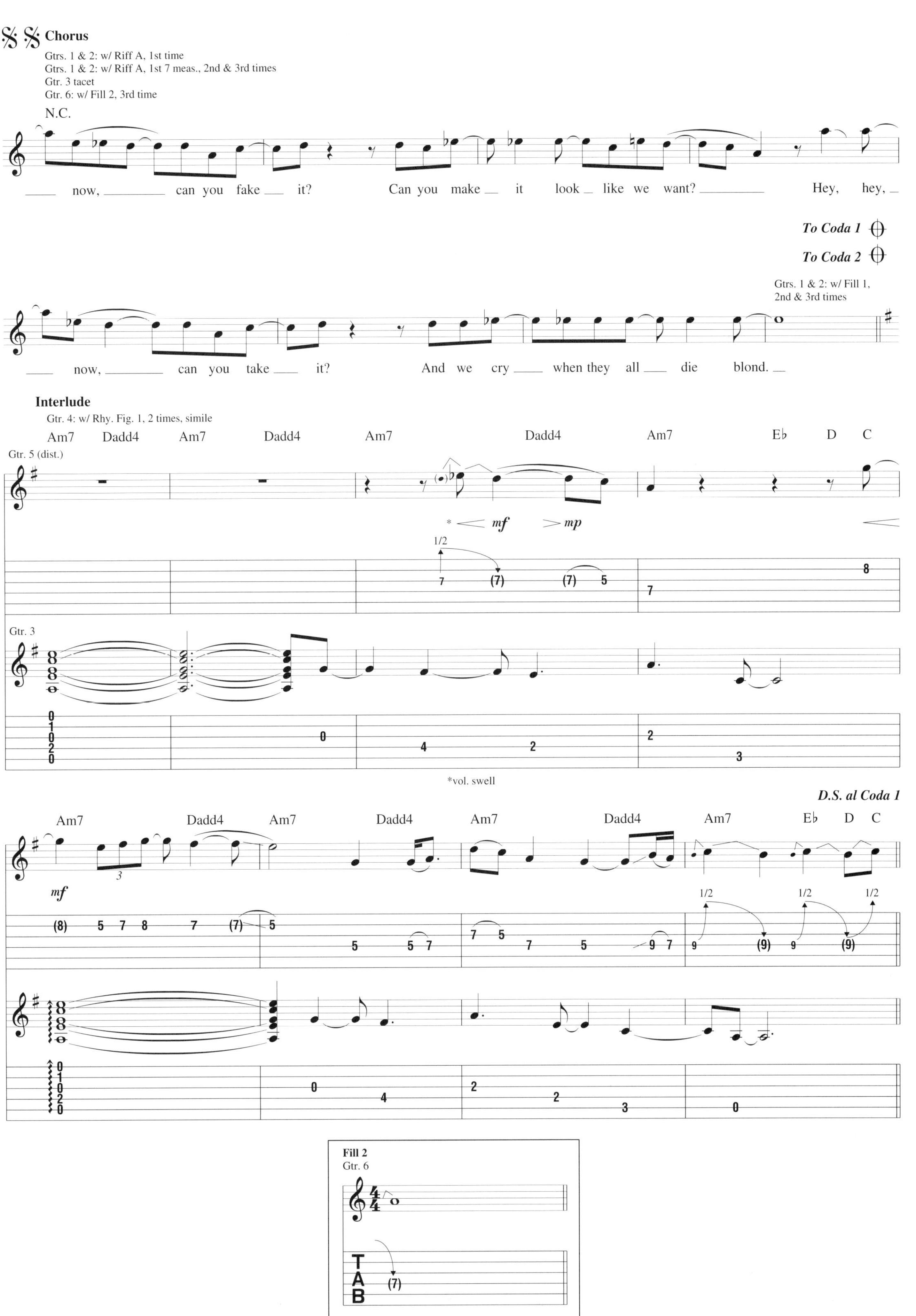

Chorus
Gtrs. 1 & 2: w/ Riff A, 1st time
Gtrs. 1 & 2: w/ Riff A, 1st 7 meas., 2nd & 3rd times
Gtr. 3 tacet
Gtr. 6: w/ Fill 2, 3rd time
N.C.
now, can you fake it? Can you make it look like we want? Hey, hey,
To Coda 1
To Coda 2
Gtrs. 1 & 2: w/ Fill 1, 2nd & 3rd times
now, can you take it? And we cry when they all die blond.
Interlude
Gtr. 4: w/ Rhy. Fig. 1, 2 times, simile
Am7 Dadd4 Am7 Dadd4 Am7 Dadd4 Am7 E♭ D C
Gtr. 5 (dist.)
Gtr. 3
*vol. swell
D.S. al Coda 1
Am7 Dadd4 Am7 Dadd4 Am7 Dadd4 Am7 E♭ D C
Fill 2
Gtr. 6

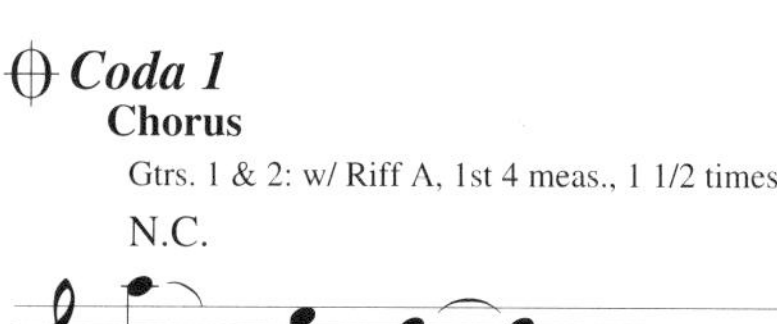
Coda 1
Chorus
Gtrs. 1 & 2: w/ Riff A, 1st 4 meas., 1 1/2 times
N.C.

Stacked dead ac - tors, stacked to the raft - ers. Line up all the bas - tards all I

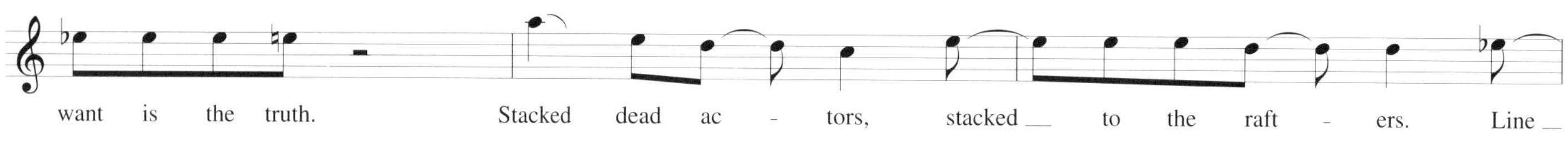
want is the truth. Stacked dead ac - tors, stacked to the raft - ers. Line

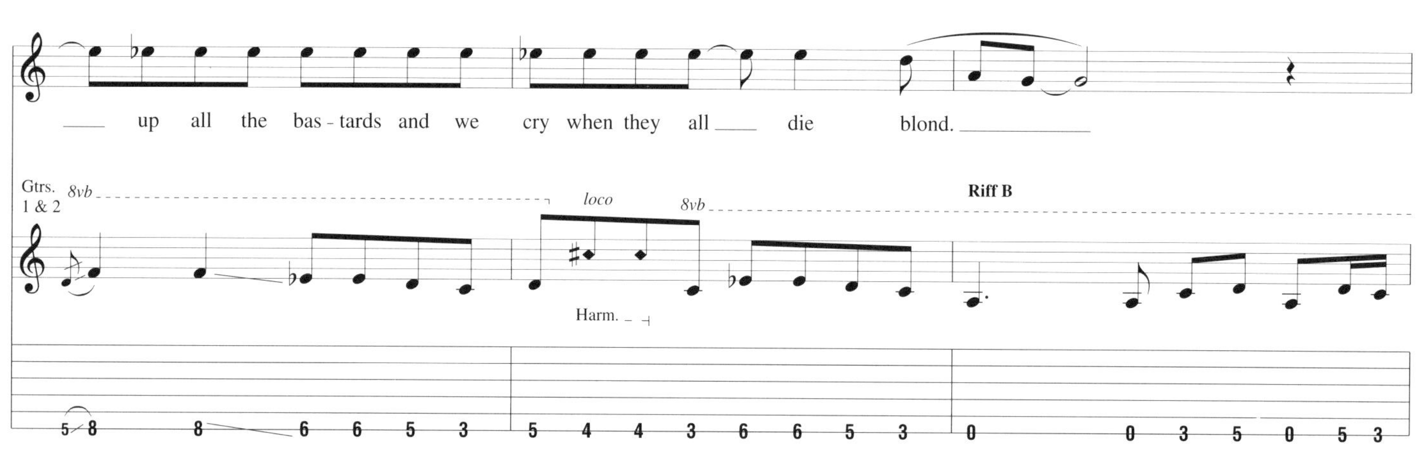
up all the bas - tards and we cry when they all die blond.
Gtrs. 1 & 2
8vb
loco
Riff B
Harm.

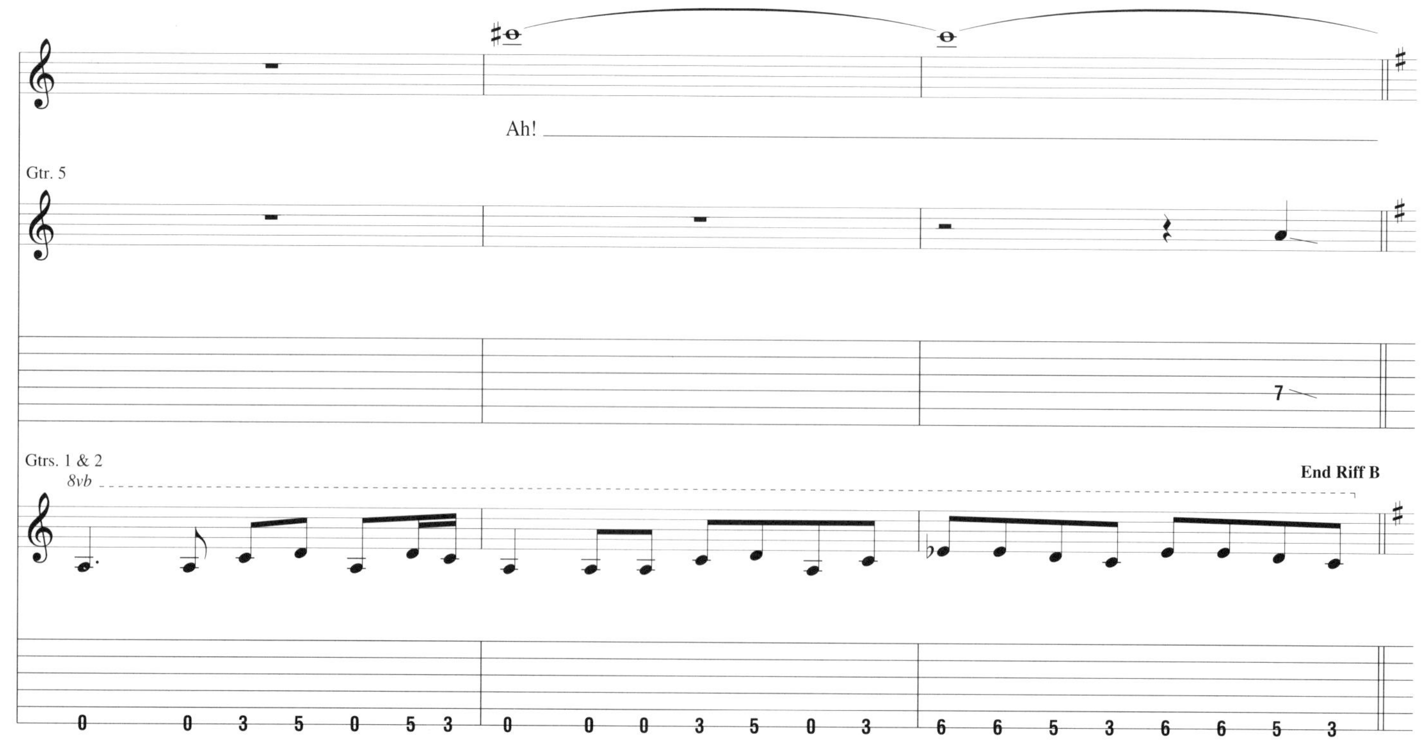
Ah!
Gtr. 5
Gtrs. 1 & 2
8vb
End Riff B

Gtrs. 1 & 2: w/ Riff B, 4 times
Gtr. 5
Gtr. 6 (dist.)
mp
full

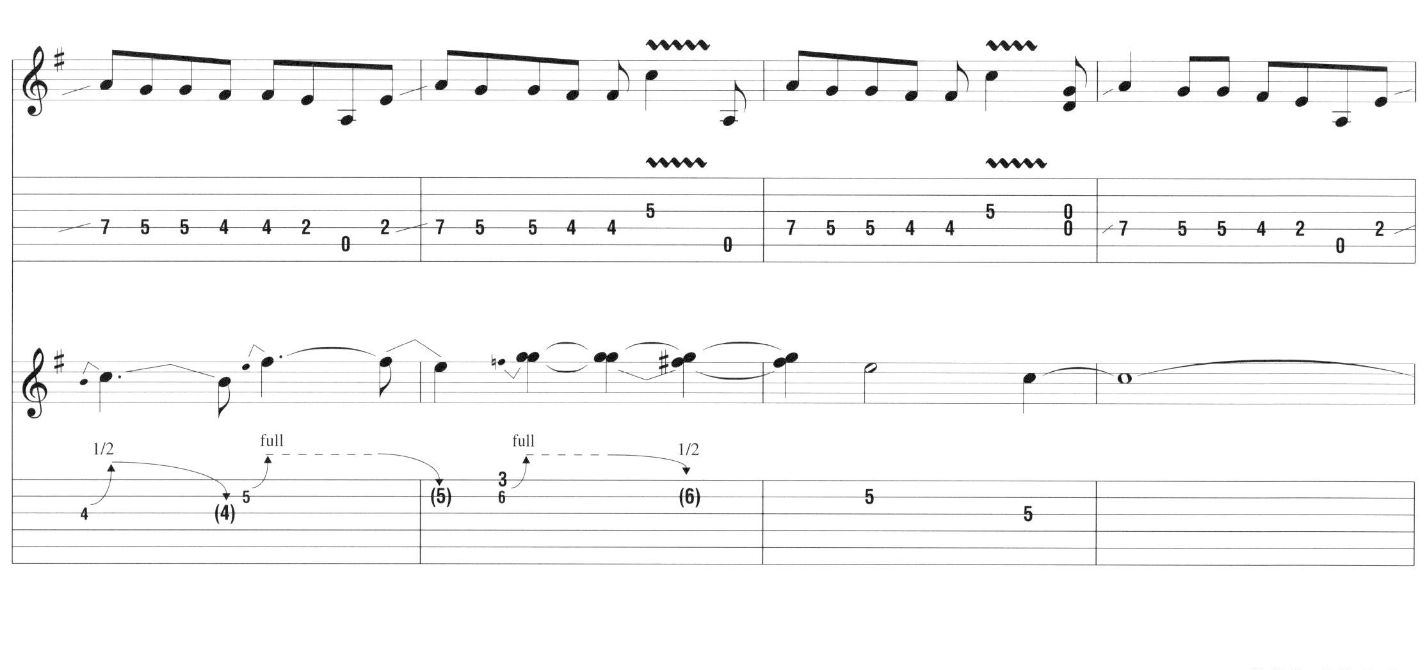
1/2
full
full
1/2

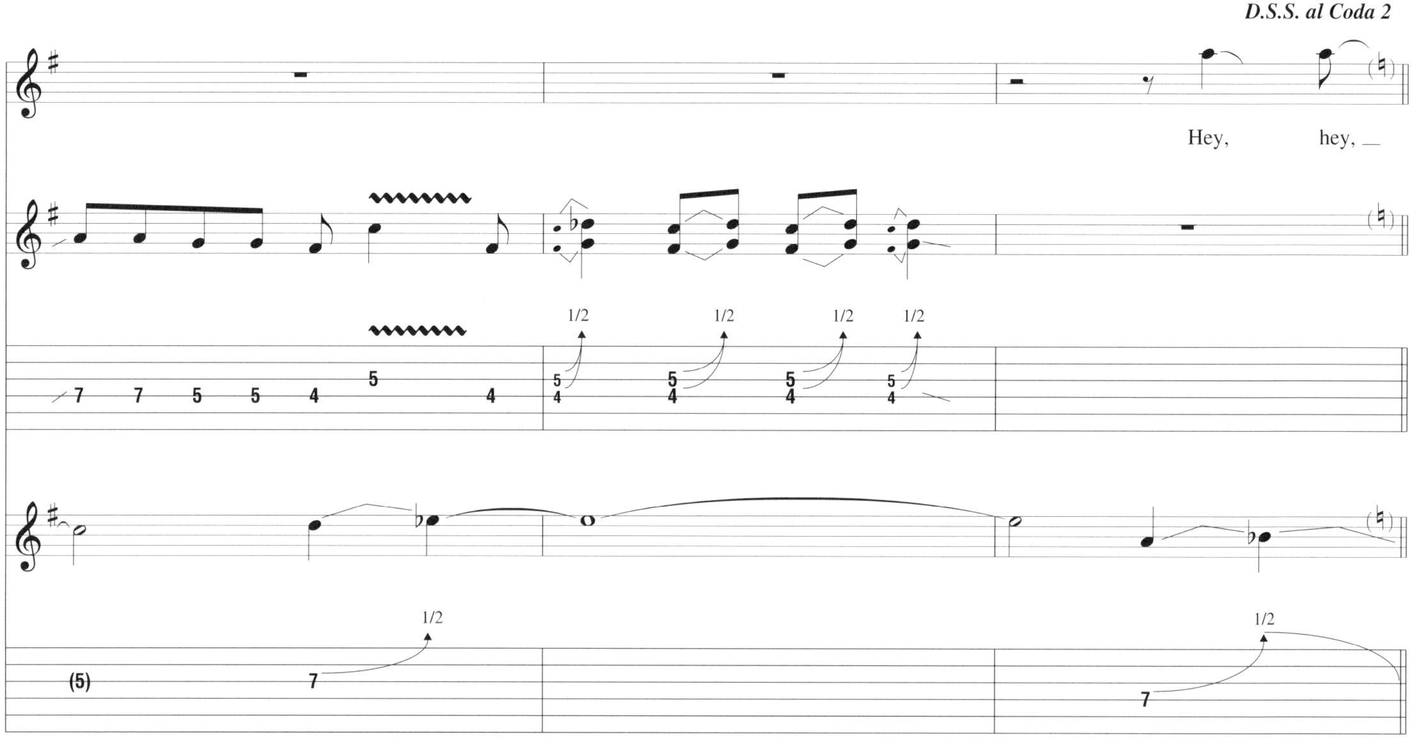
D.S.S. al Coda 2
Hey, hey,
1/2
1/2
1/2
1/2
1/2
1/2

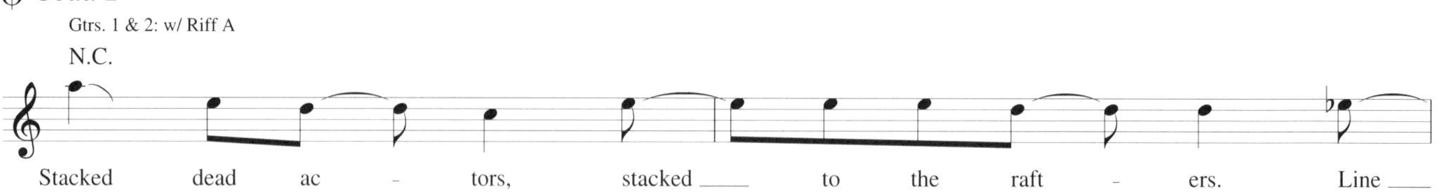
Coda 2
Gtrs. 1 & 2: w/ Riff A
N.C.
Stacked dead ac - tors, stacked to the raft - ers. Line

up all the bas - tards all I want is the truth. Stacked dead ac - tors, stacked

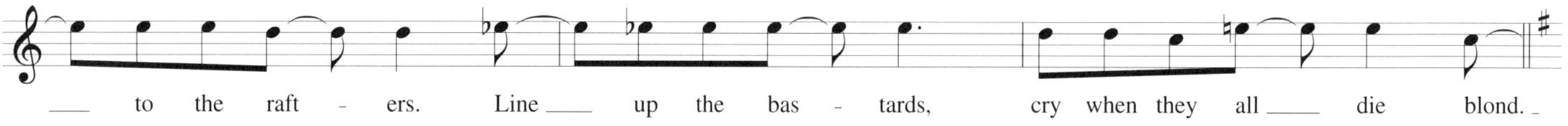
to the raft - ers. Line up the bas - tards, cry when they all die blond.

Outro
Gtr. 4: w/ Rhy. Fig. 1, 3 times, simile
Am7 Dadd4 Am7 Dadd4 Am7 Dadd4 Am7 E♭ D C Am7 Dadd4
Gtr. 5
mp
Gtr. 3
Am7 Dadd4 Am7 Dadd4 Am7 E♭ D C Am7 Dadd4
mp
full
full
Am7 Dadd4 Am7 Dadd4 Am7 E♭ D C
Gtrs. 3 & 5 tacet
Am7
Gtr. 4

Breakout

Words and Music by Dave Grohl, Nate Mendel and Taylor Hawkins

Chorus
Gtr. 1 tacet
C♯
C
N.C.
B5
Bsus4
out.
You know you make me break
out.
* Gtrs. 2 & 3 (dist.)
Rhy. Fig. 2
mf
simile on repeats
* composite arrangement
G5
A5
E5
Made me break
out.
let ring
4th time, To Coda
Em7
I don't wan - na look like that.
I don't wan - na look like that,
Bridge
no you make me break out.
Gtrs. 2 & 3
End Rhy. Fig. 2
Rhy. Fig. 3
w/ slight dist.
Gtr. 4 (dist.)
** Sing 1st time only.

Em
Em7
1.
2.
You can see
End Rhy. Fig. 3
let ring
let ring
fdbk.
fdbk.
fdbk.

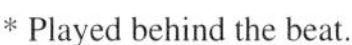
* Played behind the beat.

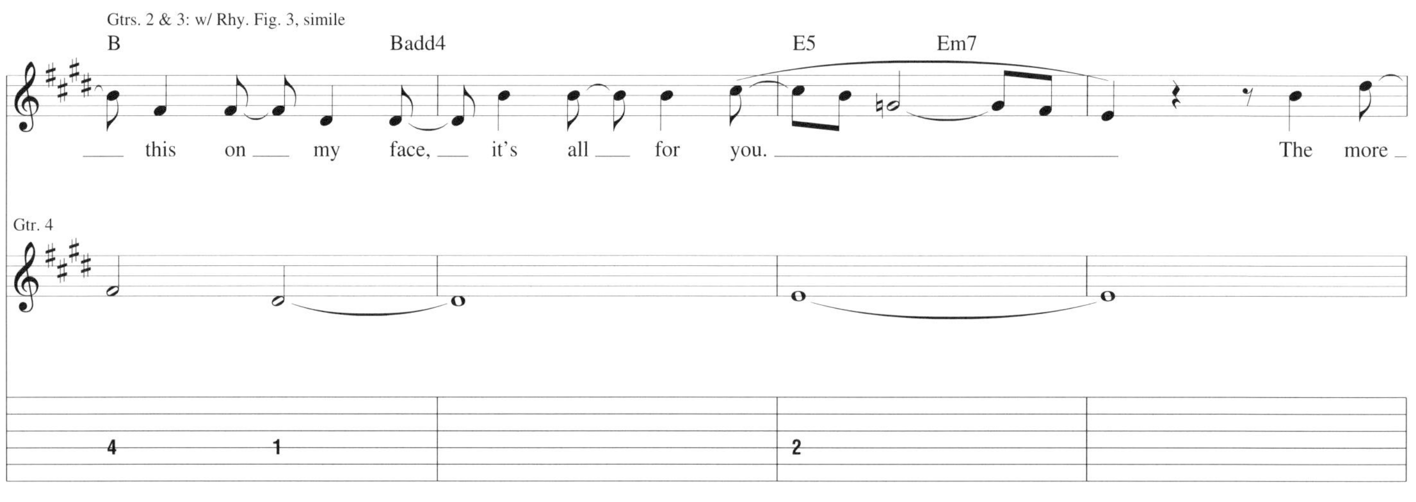
Gtrs. 2 & 3: w/ Rhy. Fig. 3, simile
B
Badd4
E5
Em7
this on my face, it's all for you. The more
Gtr. 4

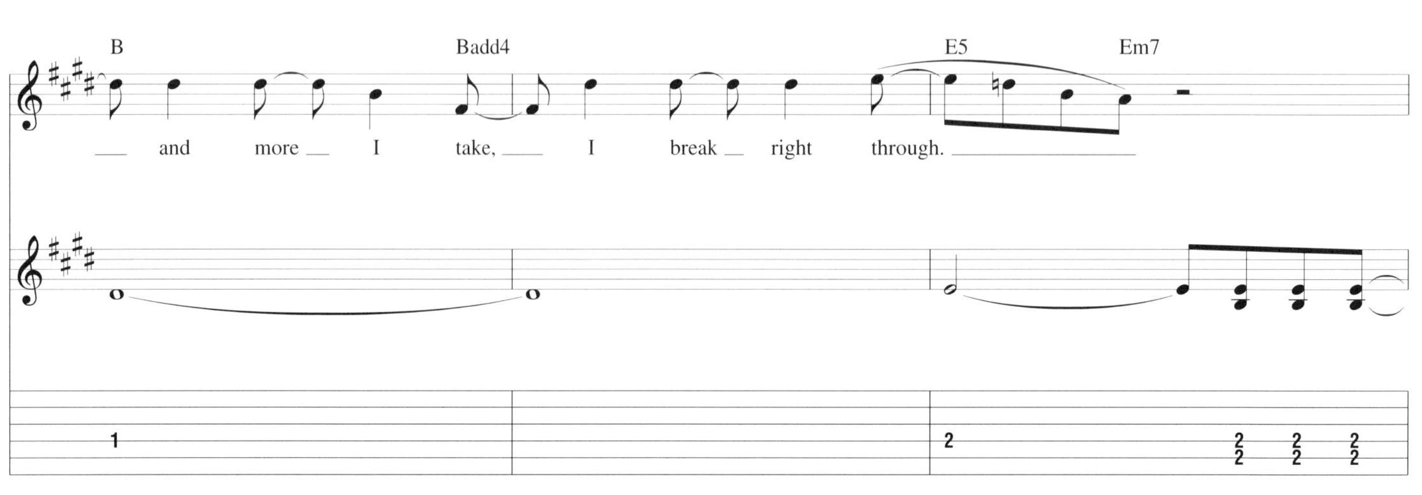
B
Badd4
E5
Em7
and more I take, I break right through.

Double-Time Feel
Gtr. 4 tacet
G5
Asus4
And ther - a - py still scares me, put me on
Gtrs. 2 & 3
w/ dist.
End Double-Time Feel
Verse
Gtr. 1: w/ Rhy. Fig. 1, 2 times, simile
Em7
E5
B
Badd4
B
my back a - gain.
2. I may be cra -
Rhy. Fig. 4
E5
C#
C#7
Cmaj7
- zy, lit - tle frayed a - round the ends. One of these
End Rhy. Fig. 4
Gtrs. 2 & 3: w/ Rhy. Fig. 4, simile
B
Badd4
B
E5
C#
C#7
days I'll phase you out.
Cmaj7
N.C.
B
N.C.
B
B7sus4
N.C.
E5/B
N.C.
E5/B
B7sus4
Burn - ing in the blast off. Burn - ing in the blast off.
Gtrs. 2 & 3
w/ dist.
P.M.

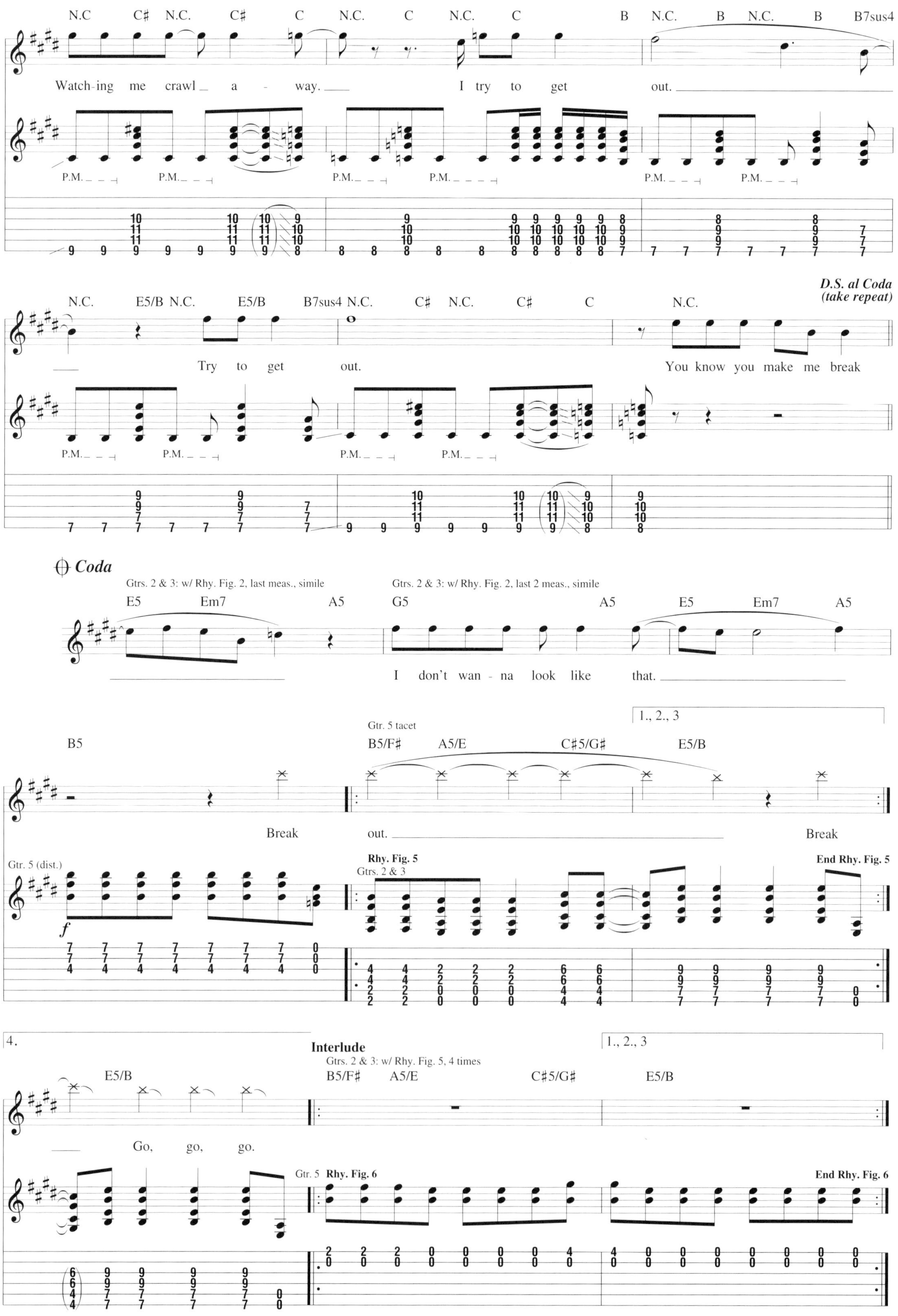
N.C C♯ N.C. C♯ C N.C. C N.C. C B N.C. B N.C. B B7sus4
Watch-ing me crawl a - way. I try to get out.
P.M.
N.C. E5/B N.C. E5/B B7sus4 N.C. C♯ N.C. C♯ C N.C.
D.S. al Coda
(take repeat)
Try to get out. You know you make me break
Coda
Gtrs. 2 & 3: w/ Rhy. Fig. 2, last meas., simile
Gtrs. 2 & 3: w/ Rhy. Fig. 2, last 2 meas., simile
E5 Em7 A5 G5 A5 E5 Em7 A5
I don't wan - na look like that.
1., 2., 3
Gtr. 5 tacet
B5 B5/F♯ A5/E C♯5/G♯ E5/B
Break out. Break
Gtr. 5 (dist.)
Rhy. Fig. 5
Gtrs. 2 & 3
End Rhy. Fig. 5
4.
Interlude
Gtrs. 2 & 3: w/ Rhy. Fig. 5, 4 times
E5/B B5/F♯ A5/E C♯5/G♯ E5/B
Go, go, go.
Gtr. 5 Rhy. Fig. 6
End Rhy. Fig. 6

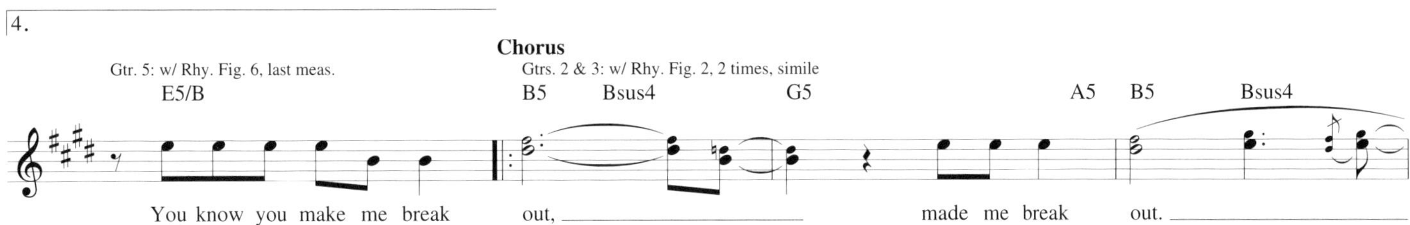
4.
Chorus
Gtr. 5: w/ Rhy. Fig. 6, last meas.
Gtrs. 2 & 3: w/ Rhy. Fig. 2, 2 times, simile
E5/B
B5 Bsus4 G5 A5 B5 Bsus4
You know you make me break out, made me break out.

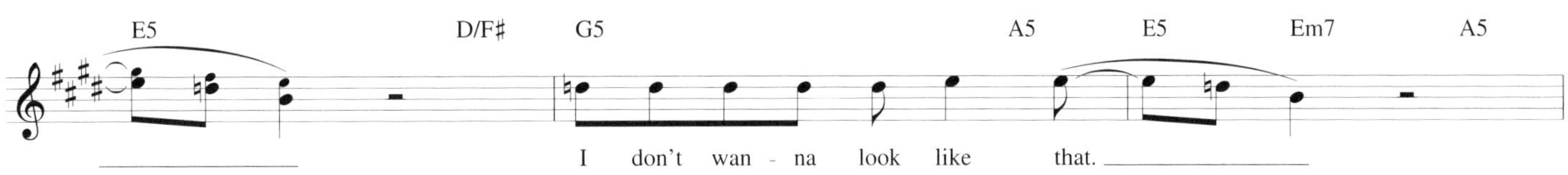
E5 D/F# G5 A5 E5 Em7 A5
I don't wan - na look like that.

1.
2.
G5 A5 E5 Em7 A5 E5 Em7 A5
I don't wan - na look like that, no you make me break

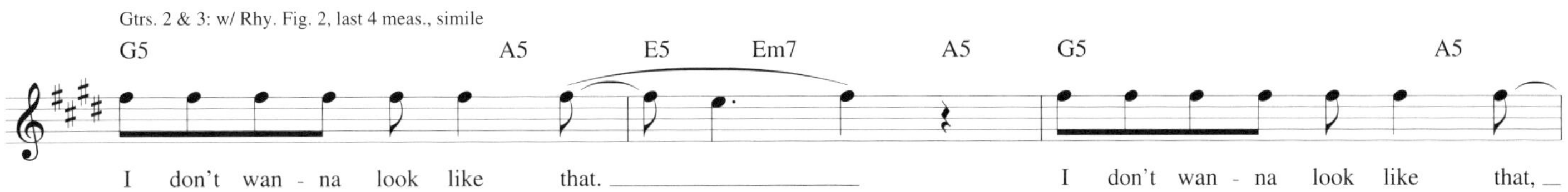
Gtrs. 2 & 3: w/ Rhy. Fig. 2, last 4 meas., simile
G5 A5 E5 Em7 A5 G5 A5
I don't wan - na look like that. I don't wan - na look like that,

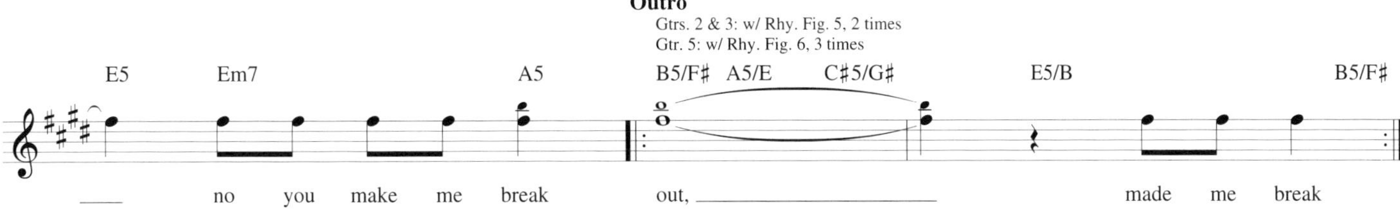
Outro
Gtrs. 2 & 3: w/ Rhy. Fig. 5, 2 times
Gtr. 5: w/ Rhy. Fig. 6, 3 times
E5 Em7 A5 B5/F# A5/E C#5/G# E5/B B5/F#
no you make me break out, made me break

A5/E C#5/G# E5/B B5/F# A5/E C#5/G# E5/B
out, yeah.
Gtrs. 2 & 3

Learn to Fly

Words and Music by Dave Grohl, Nate Mendel and Taylor Hawkins

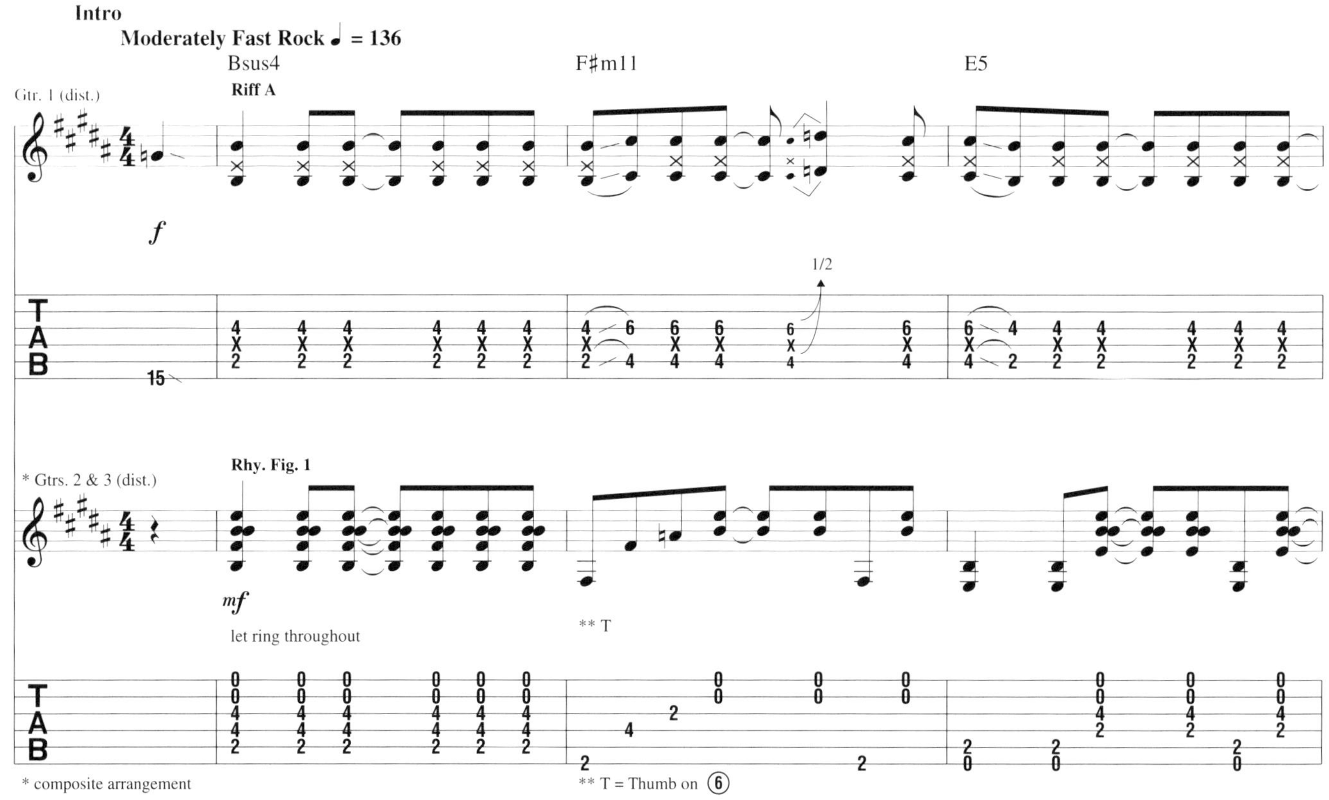

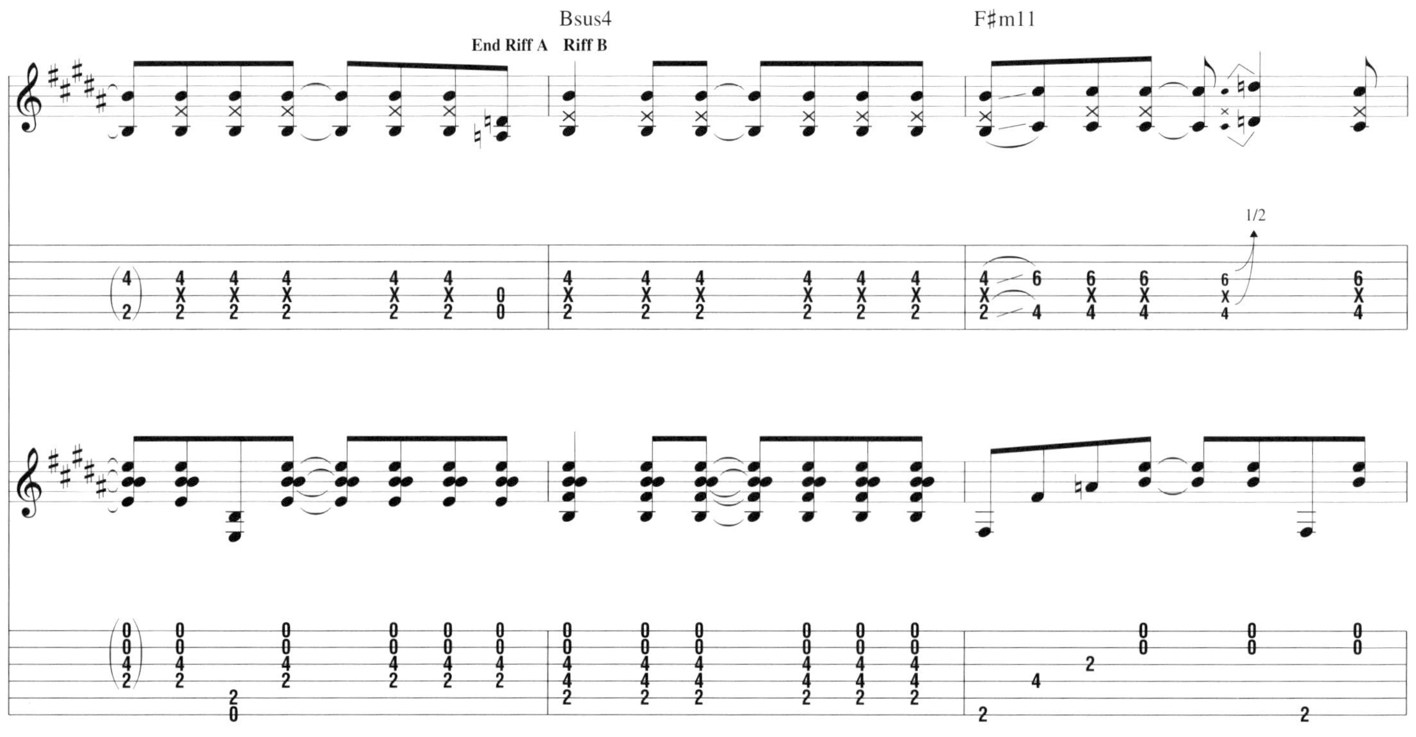

E5
Verse
Bsus2
1. Run and tell all of the an-
End Riff B
Fill 1
let ring
End Rhy. Fig. 1
Riff C
F♯m11
E5
-gels, this could take all night.
End Fill 1
End Riff C
T
Gtrs. 2 & 3: w/ Riff C, 2 1/2 times, simile
Gtr. 1 tacet
Bsus2
F♯m11
E5
Think-in' it in time will help me get things right.

Bsus2
F♯m11
E5
Hook me up a new rev - o - lu - tion, 'cause this one is a lie.

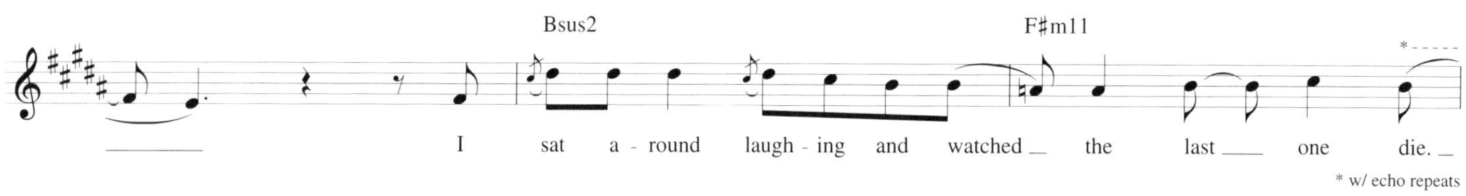
Bsus2
F♯m11
I sat a - round laugh - ing and watched the last one die.
* w/ echo repeats

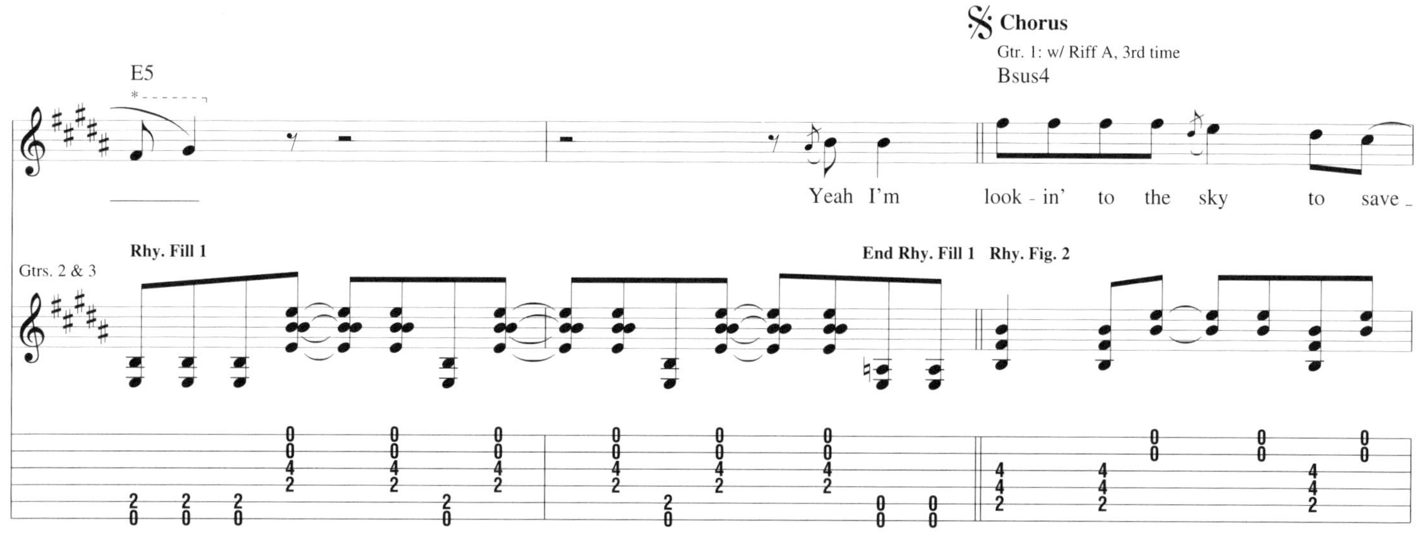
E5
Chorus
Gtr. 1: w/ Riff A, 3rd time
Bsus4
Yeah I'm look - in' to the sky to save
Gtrs. 2 & 3
Rhy. Fill 1
End Rhy. Fill 1
Rhy. Fig. 2

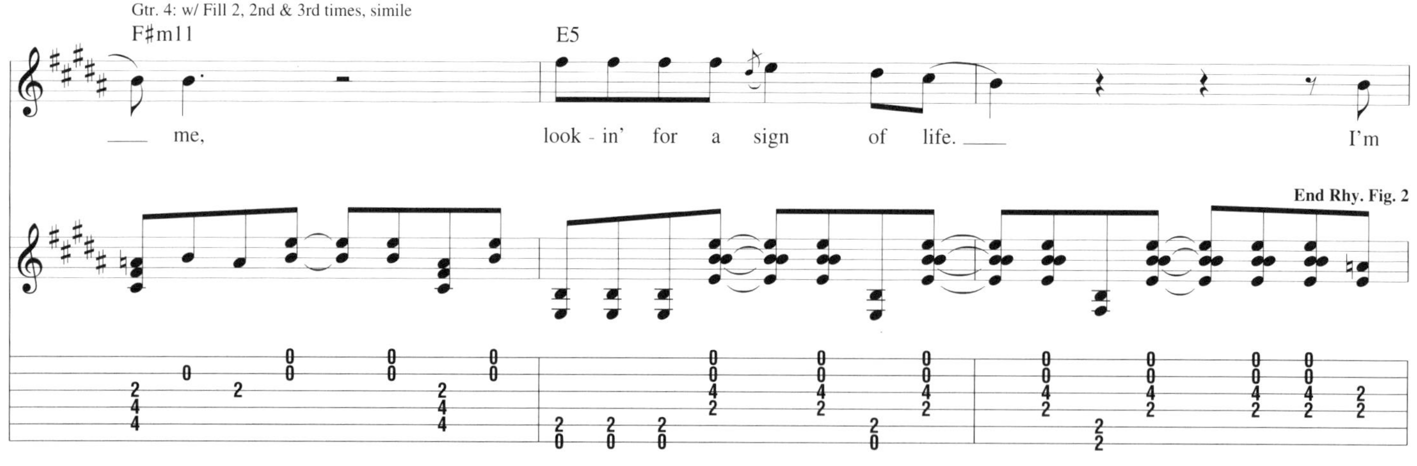
Gtr. 4: w/ Fill 2, 2nd & 3rd times, simile
F♯m11
E5
me, look - in' for a sign of life. I'm
End Rhy. Fig. 2

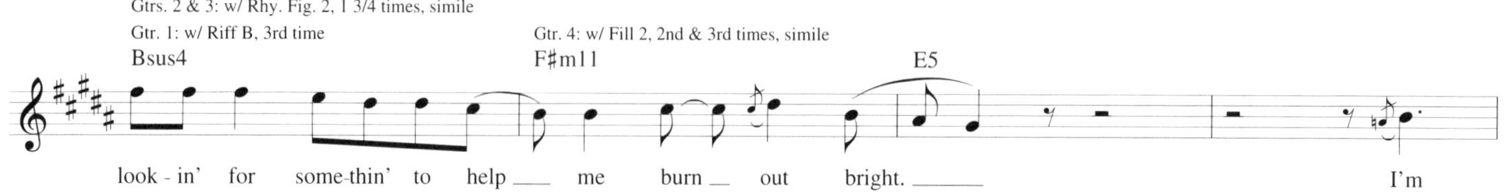
Gtrs. 2 & 3: w/ Rhy. Fig. 2, 1 3/4 times, simile
Gtr. 1: w/ Riff B, 3rd time
Bsus4
Gtr. 4: w/ Fill 2, 2nd & 3rd times, simile
F♯m11
E5
look - in' for some - thin' to help me burn out bright. I'm

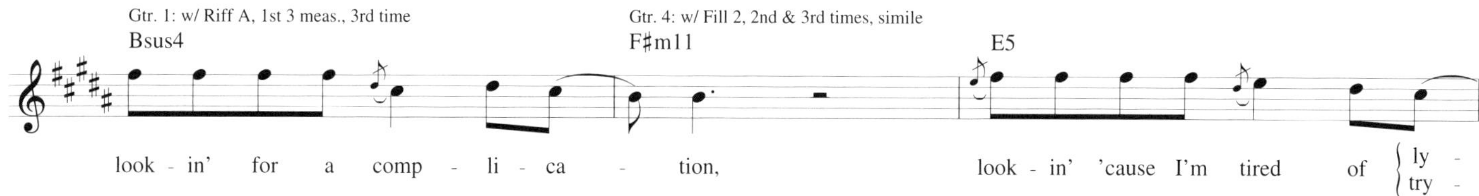
Gtr. 1: w/ Riff A, 1st 3 meas., 3rd time
Bsus4
Gtr. 4: w/ Fill 2, 2nd & 3rd times, simile
F♯m11
E5
look - in' for a comp - li - ca - tion, look - in' 'cause I'm tired of ly - try -

Fill 3

Gtr. 1

steady gliss.

Verse
Gtr. 1: w/ Fill 1
Gtr. 2: w/ Riff C, 3 1/2 times, simile
Gtr. 4 tacet
* Badd9
F♯m11
Esus2
think I'm dy - in' mis-sing pa - tience, it can wait one night.
Gtr. 3
Riff D
End Riff D
* Chord symbols reflect combined tonality.
Gtr. 3: w/ Riff D, 2 1/2 times
Badd9
F♯m11
Esus2
Give it all a - way if you give me one last try.
* w/ echo repeats
Badd9
F♯m11
We'll live hap - pi - ly ev - er trapped if you
Esus2
Badd9
just save my life. Run - nin' down the an - gels and ev -
D.S. al Coda 1
Gtrs. 2 & 3: w/ Rhy. Fill 1, simile
F♯m11
E5
'ry - thing's all right. I'm
Coda 1
G
Asus4
A
Make my way back home when I learn to fly
Rhy. Fig. 3
Gtrs. 2 & 3

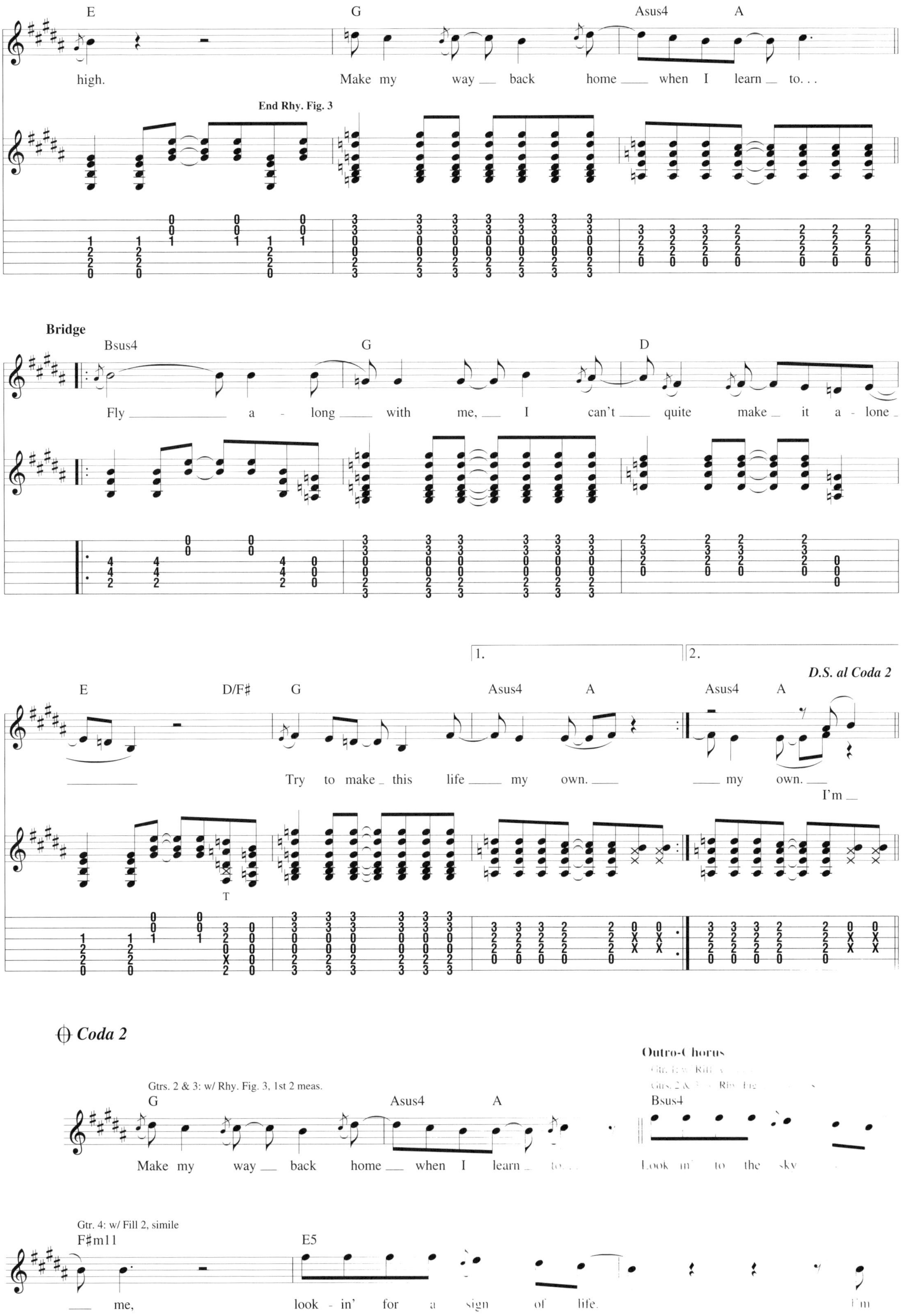

E G Asus4 A

high. Make my way back home when I learn to...

End Rhy. Fig. 3

Bridge

Bsus4 G D

Fly along with me, I can't quite make it alone

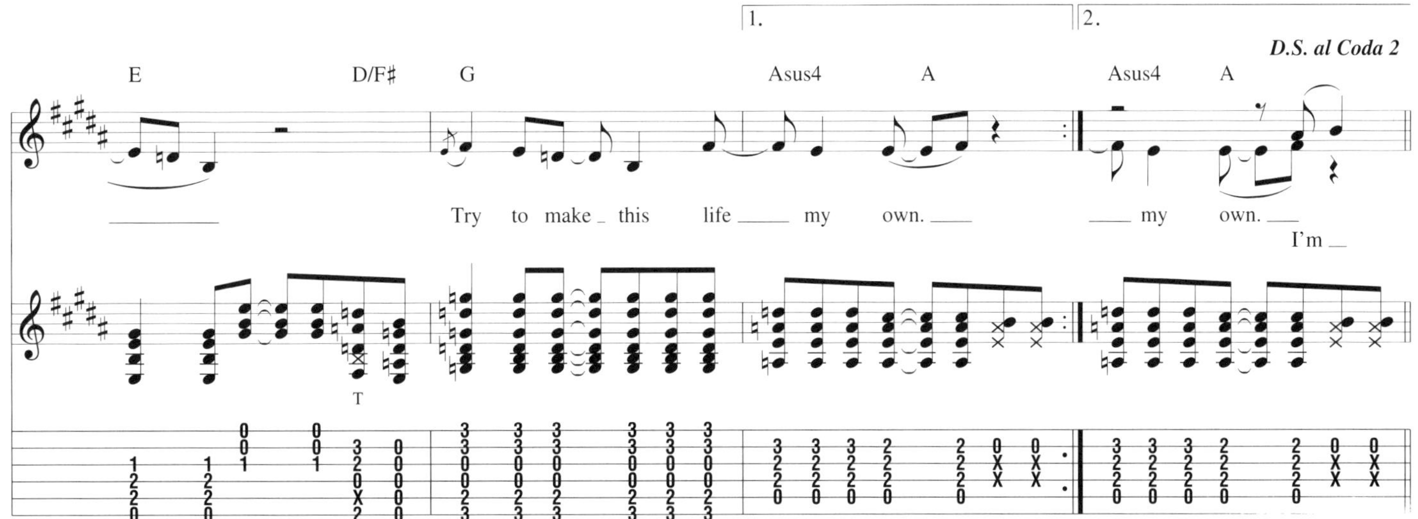

Coda 2

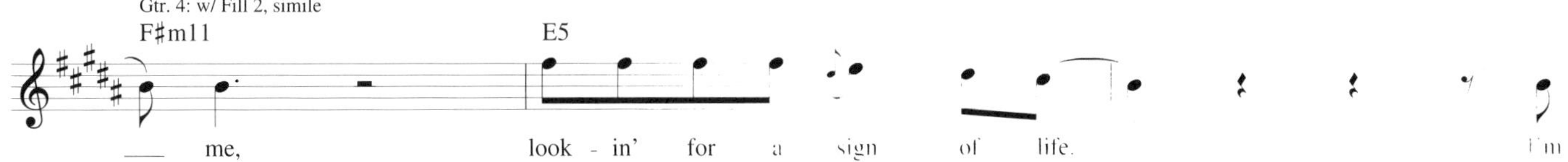

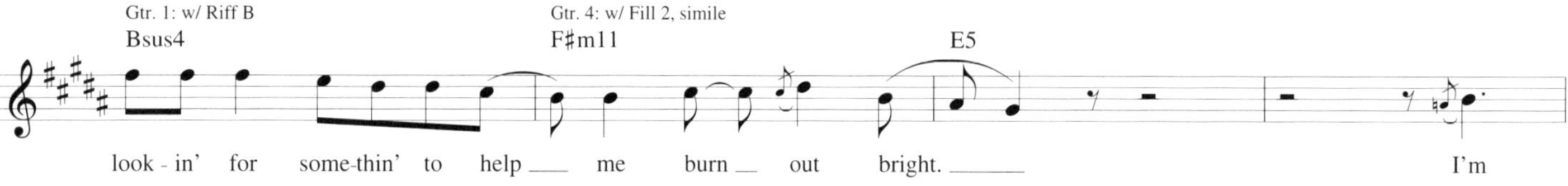
Gtr. 1: w/ Riff B
Bsus4
Gtr. 4: w/ Fill 2, simile
F♯m11
E5
look - in' for some-thin' to help ___ me burn __ out bright. ______
I'm

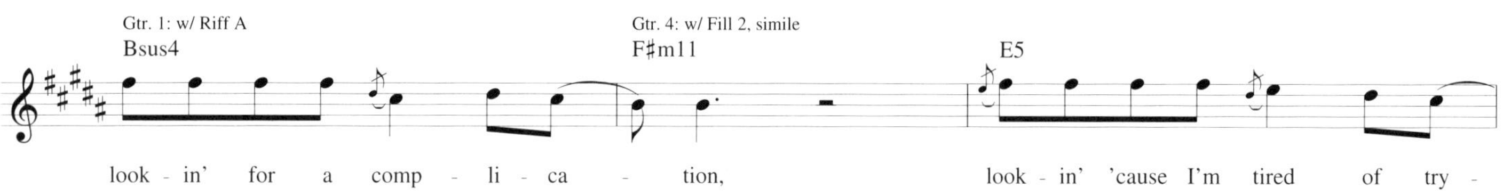
Gtr. 1: w/ Riff A
Bsus4
Gtr. 4: w/ Fill 2, simile
F♯m11
E5
look - in' for a comp - li - ca - tion,
look - in' 'cause I'm tired of try -

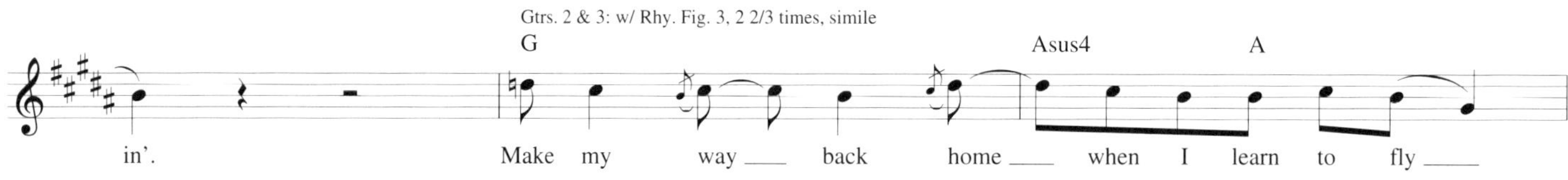
Gtrs. 2 & 3: w/ Rhy. Fig. 3, 2 2/3 times, simile
G
Asus4
A
in'.
Make my way ___ back home ___ when I learn to fly _____

E
G
Asus4
A
high.
Make my way ___ back home ___ when I learn to fly.

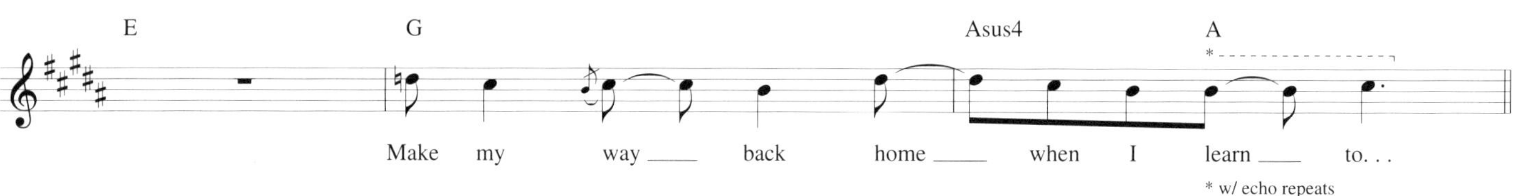
E
G
Asus4
A
Make my way ____ back home ____ when I learn ____ to. . .
* w/ echo repeats

Outro

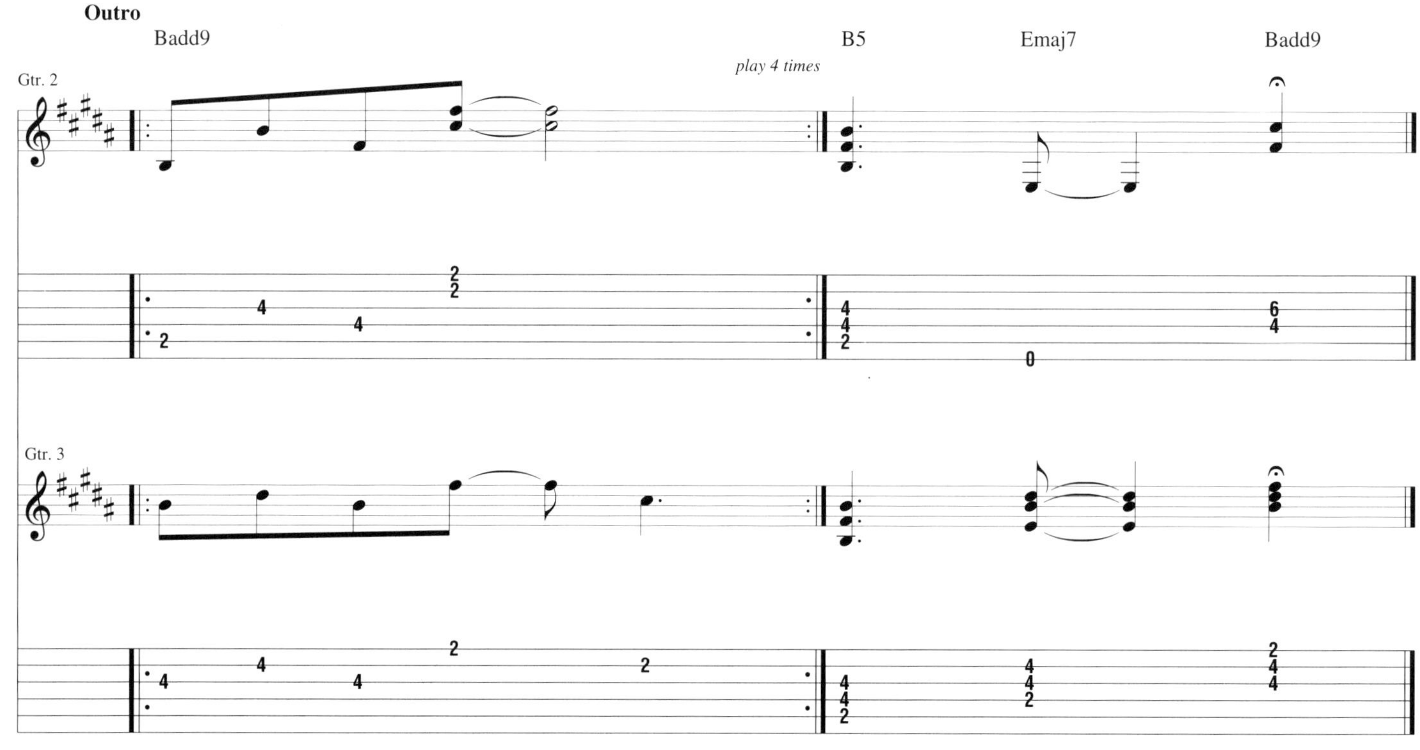
Badd9
B5
Emaj7
Badd9
play 4 times
Gtr. 2
Gtr. 3

Gimme Stitches

Words and Music by Dave Grohl, Nate Mendel and Taylor Hawkins

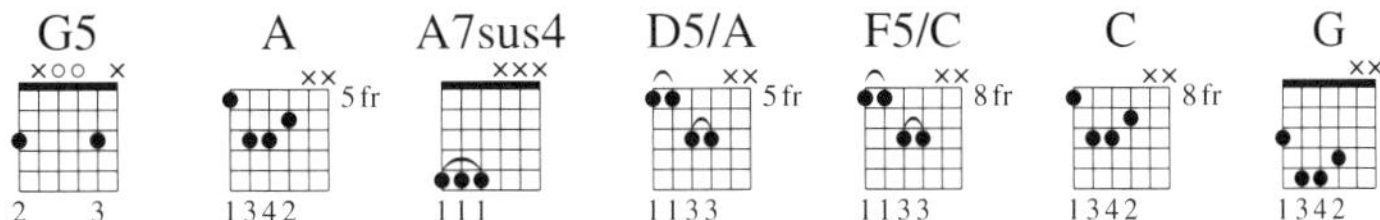

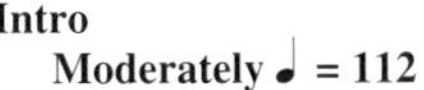

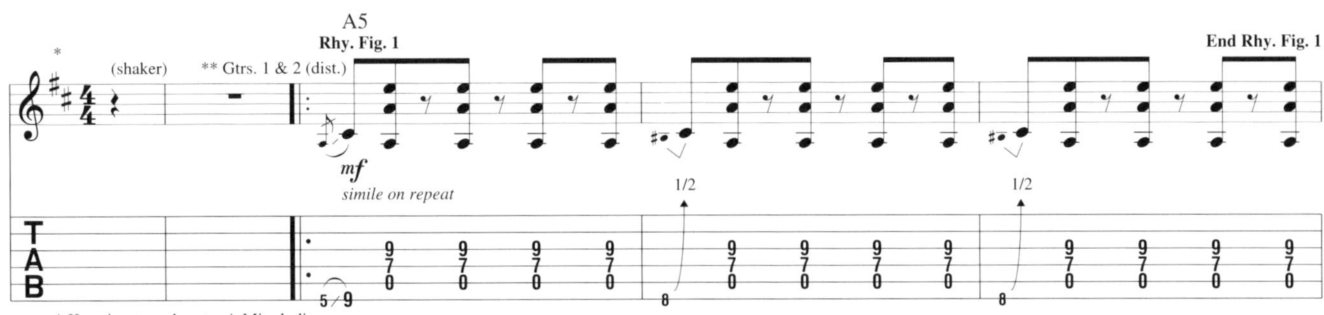

* Key signature denotes A Mixolydian.

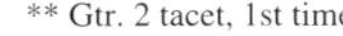

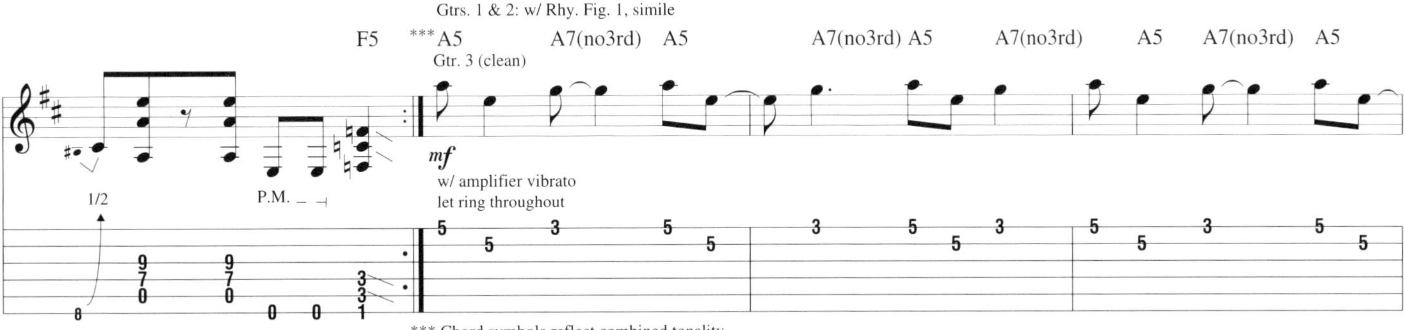

*** Chord symbols reflect combined tonality.

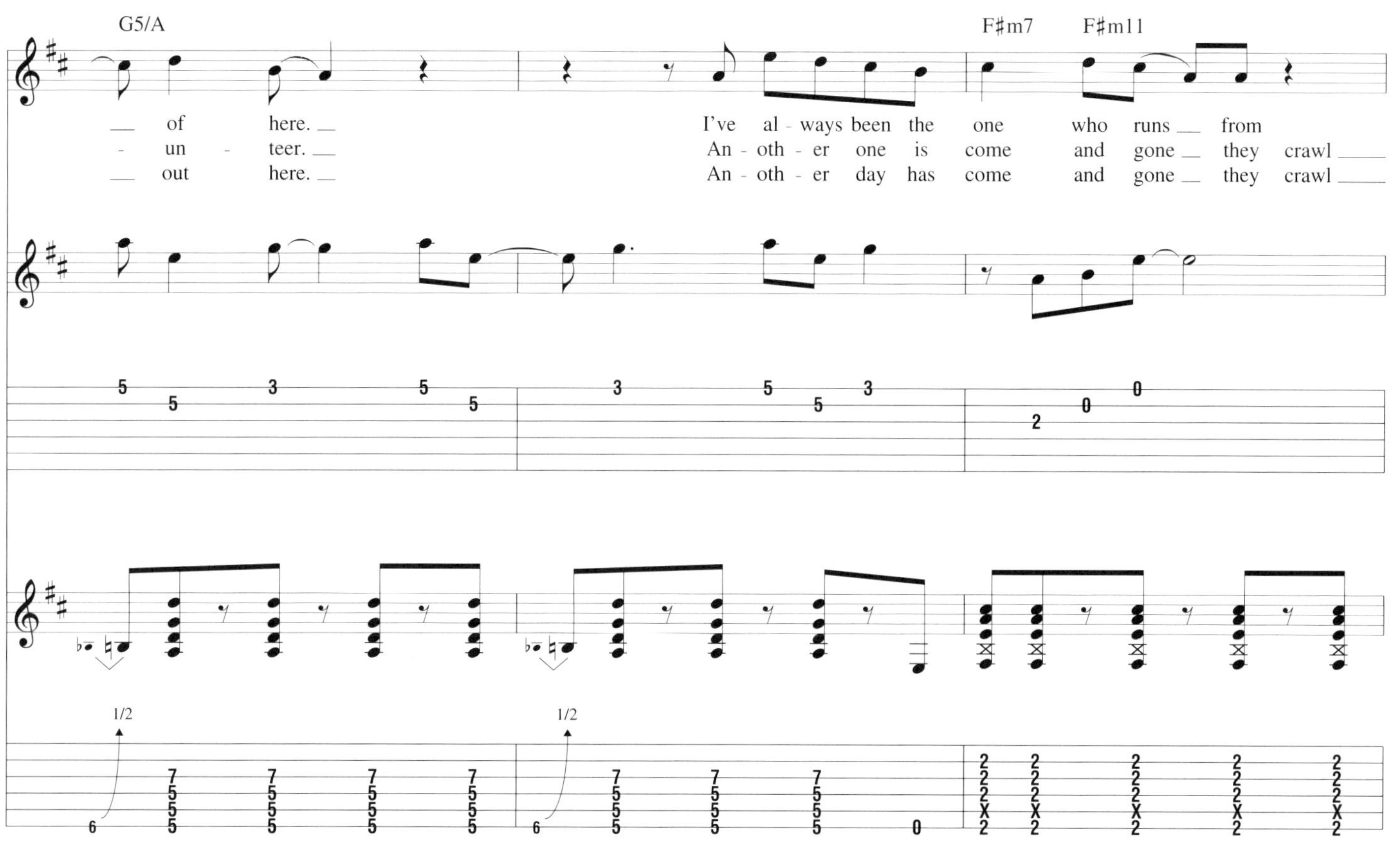

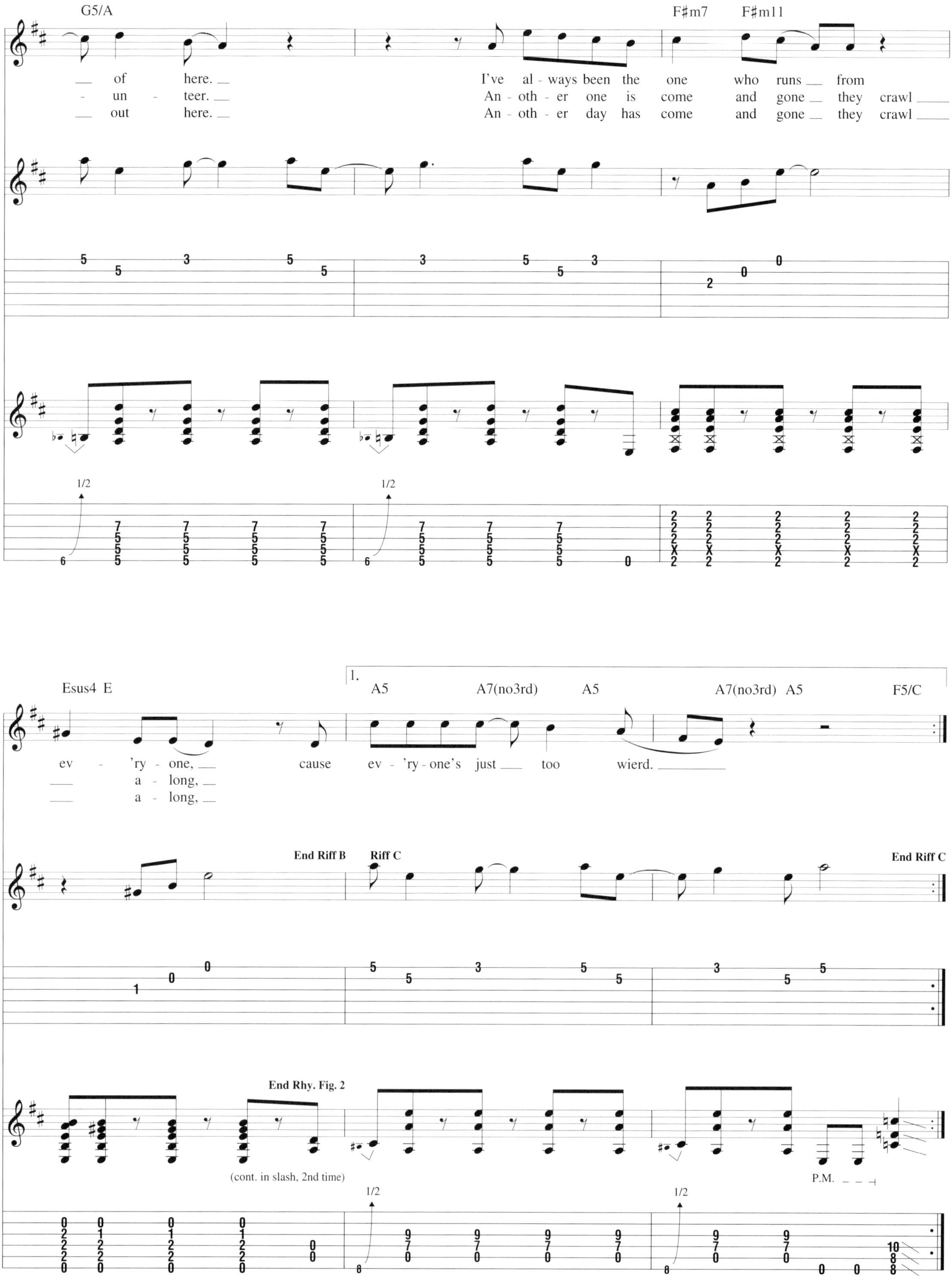

Esus4 E

1.

A5 A7(no3rd) A5 A7(no3rd) A5 F5/C

ev - 'ry - one, cause ev - 'ry - one's just too wierd.

a - long,

a - long,

End Riff B

Riff C

End Riff C

End Rhy. Fig. 2

(cont. in slash, 2nd time)

1/2

1/2

P.M.

2.
Chorus
Bkgd. Voc.: w/ Voc. Fig. 1, 1 3/4 times, 3rd time
Gtrs. 1 & 2: w/ Rhy. Fig. 7, 2 times, 3rd time, simile
G5
E G♯ E
A
A7sus4
Rhy. Fig. 3
End Rhy. Fig. 3
Rhy. Fig. 4
Gtrs. 1 & 2
simile on repeat
make them dis - ap - pear.
wast - in' all these years.
Dress me up in stitch - es it's now
Gtr. 3
Riff D
End Riff D
Riff E
D5/A
F5/C
C
E G E
End Rhy. Fig. 4
or nev - er, tired of wear - ing black and blue.
End Riff E
To Coda 2
To Coda 1
Gtrs. 1 & 2: w/ Rhy. Fig. 4, 1st & 2nd times, simile
Gtr. 3: w/ Riff E, 1st & 2nd times, simile
*A
Dsus2/A
Fsus2/C
Dress me up in stitch - es it's now or nev - er dying to get my blood on you,
* Chord symbols reflect combined tonality.
Gtr. 3: w/ Riff C, simile
C
G
A5
A7(no3rd)
A5
A7(no3rd)
F5/C
Blood on you.
Gtrs. 1 & 2
P.M.

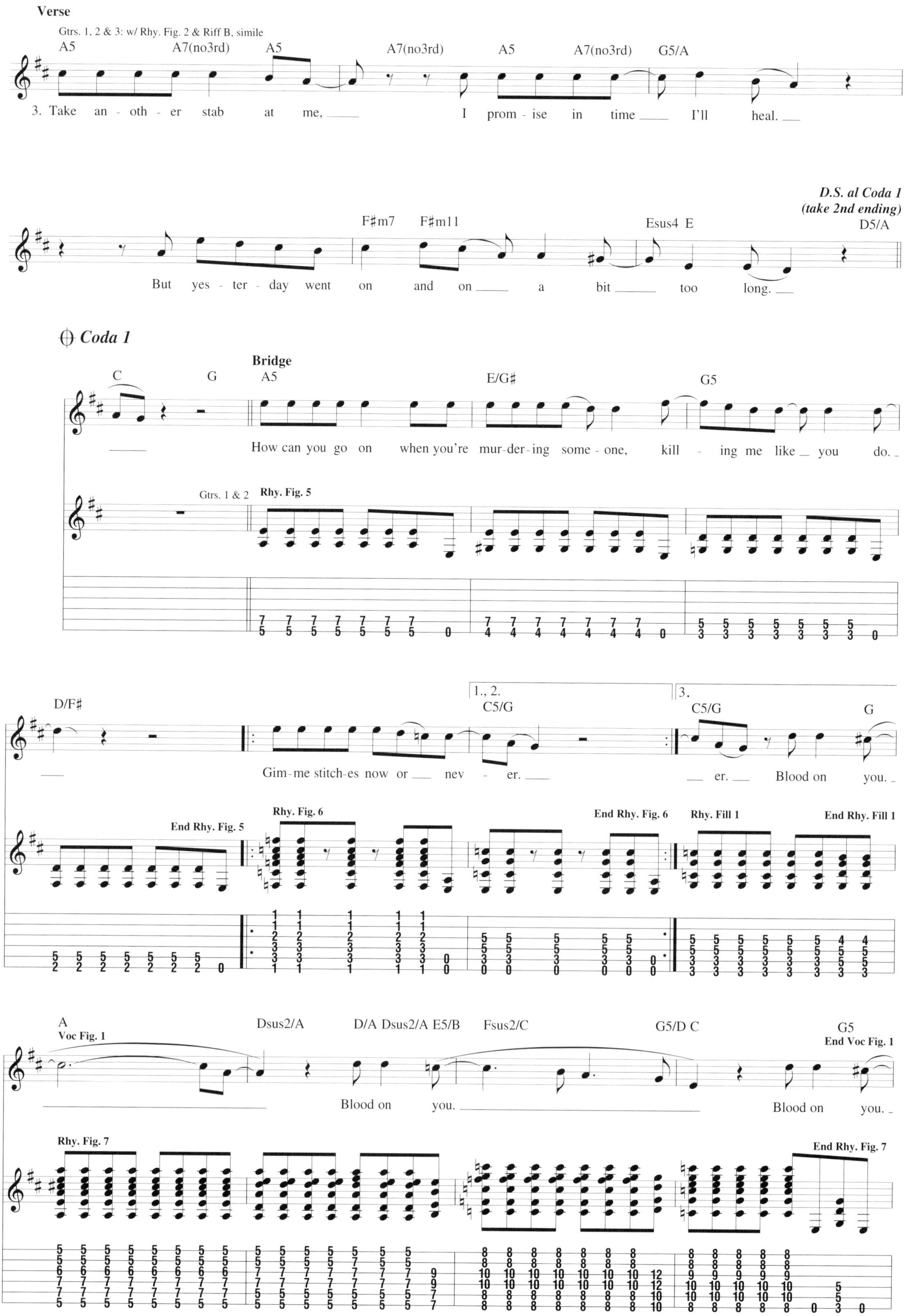
Verse
Gtrs. 1, 2 & 3: w/ Rhy. Fig. 2 & Riff B, simile
A5 A7(no3rd) A5 A7(no3rd) A5 A7(no3rd) G5/A
3. Take an - oth - er stab at me, I prom - ise in time I'll heal.
D.S. al Coda 1
(take 2nd ending)
F♯m7 F♯m11 Esus4 E D5/A
But yes - ter - day went on and on a bit too long.
Coda 1
Bridge
C G A5 E/G♯ G5
How can you go on when you're mur-der-ing some - one, kill - ing me like you do.
Gtrs. 1 & 2
Rhy. Fig. 5
D/F♯
1., 2.
C5/G
3.
C5/G G
Gim-me stitch-es now or nev - er. er. Blood on you.
End Rhy. Fig. 5
Rhy. Fig. 6
End Rhy. Fig. 6
Rhy. Fill 1
End Rhy. Fill 1
A Dsus2/A D/A Dsus2/A E5/B Fsus2/C G5/D C G5
Voc Fig. 1
End Voc Fig. 1
Blood on you. Blood on you.
Rhy. Fig. 7
End Rhy. Fig. 7

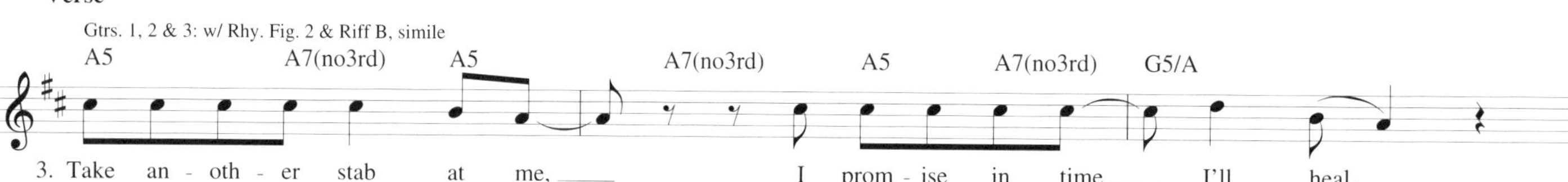

D.S.S. al Coda 2

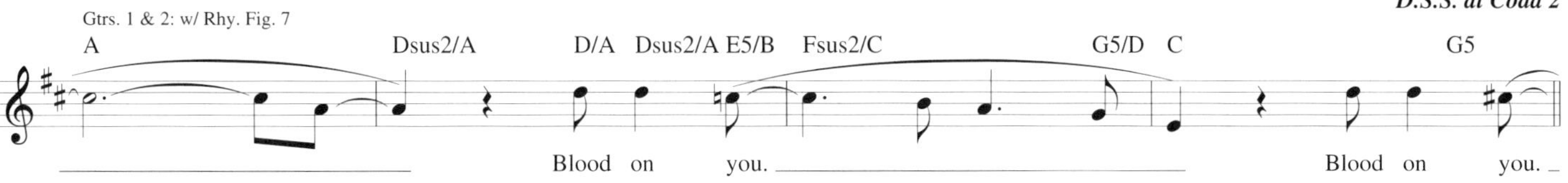
Gtrs. 1 & 2: w/ Rhy. Fig. 7
A
Dsus2/A
D/A Dsus2/A E5/B
Fsus2/C
G5/D C
G5
Blood on you.
Blood on you.

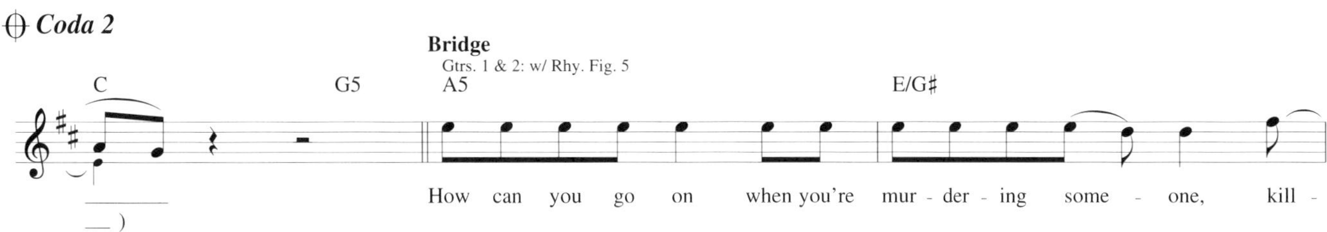
Coda 2
Bridge
Gtrs. 1 & 2: w/ Rhy. Fig. 5
C
G5
A5
E/G♯
)
How can you go on when you're mur - der - ing some - one, kill -

Gtrs. 1 & 2: w/ Rhy. Fig. 6, 3 1/2 times, simile
G5
D/F♯
F
C5/G
play 3 times
- ing me like you do.
Gim - me stitch - es now or nev - er.
Gtr. 4 (dist.)
mf
simile on repeats
1/2
1/2

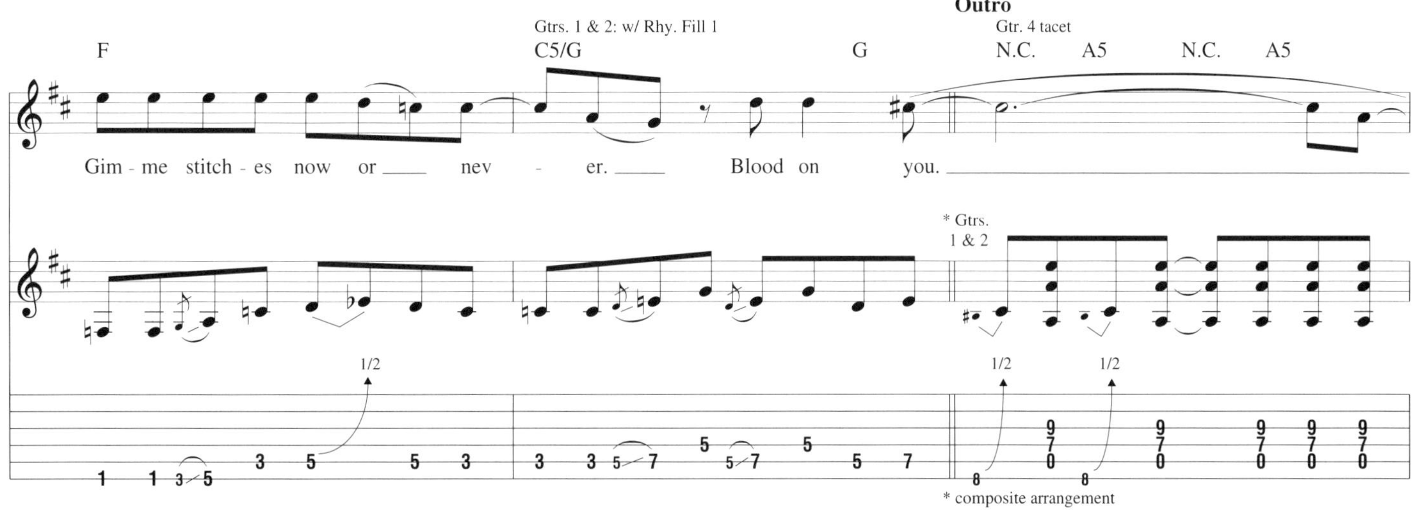
Outro
Gtrs. 1 & 2: w/ Rhy. Fill 1
Gtr. 4 tacet
F
C5/G
G
N.C. A5 N.C. A5
Gim - me stitch - es now or nev - er. Blood on you.
* Gtrs. 1 & 2
1/2
* composite arrangement

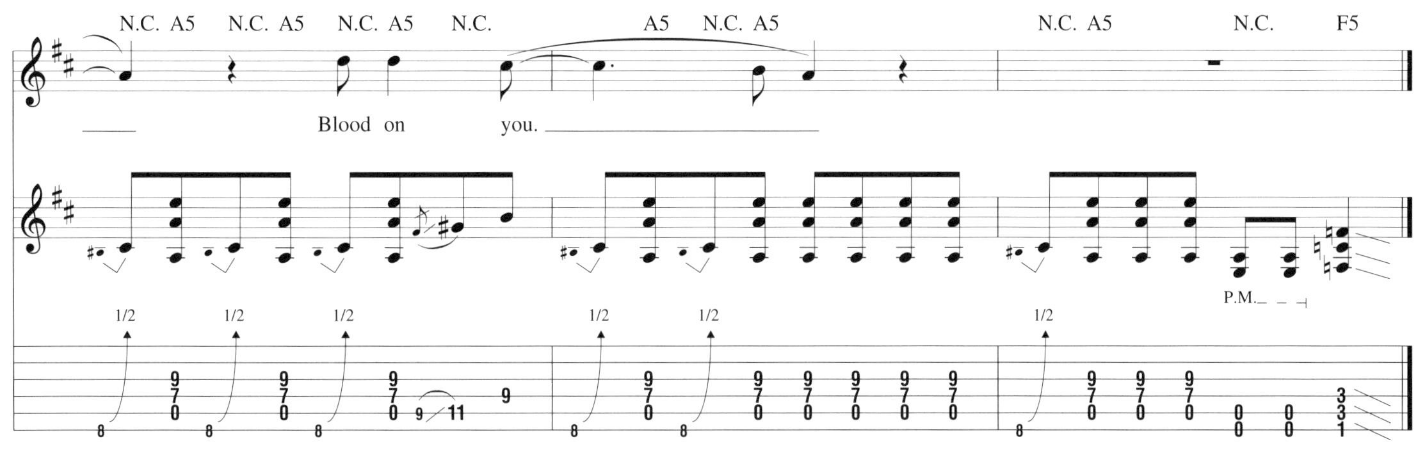
N.C. A5 N.C. A5 N.C. A5 N.C.
A5 N.C. A5
N.C. A5
N.C. F5
Blood on you.
P.M.
1/2

Generator

Words and Music by Dave Grohl, Nate Mendel and Taylor Hawkins

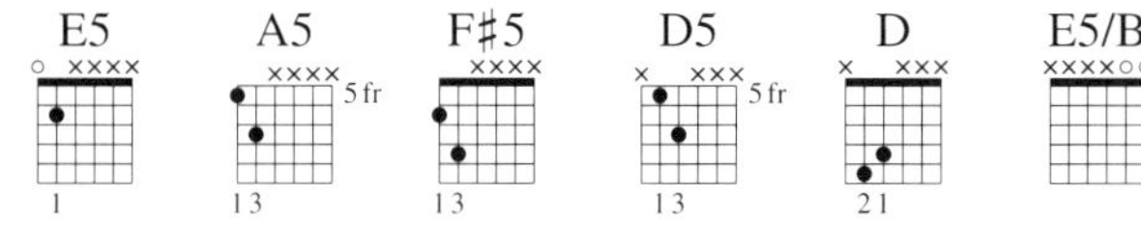

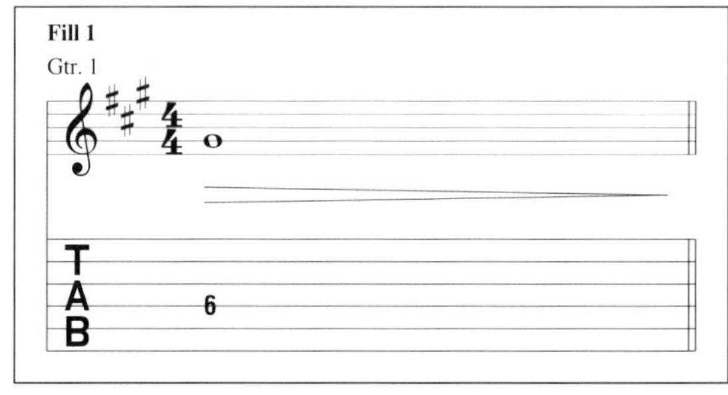

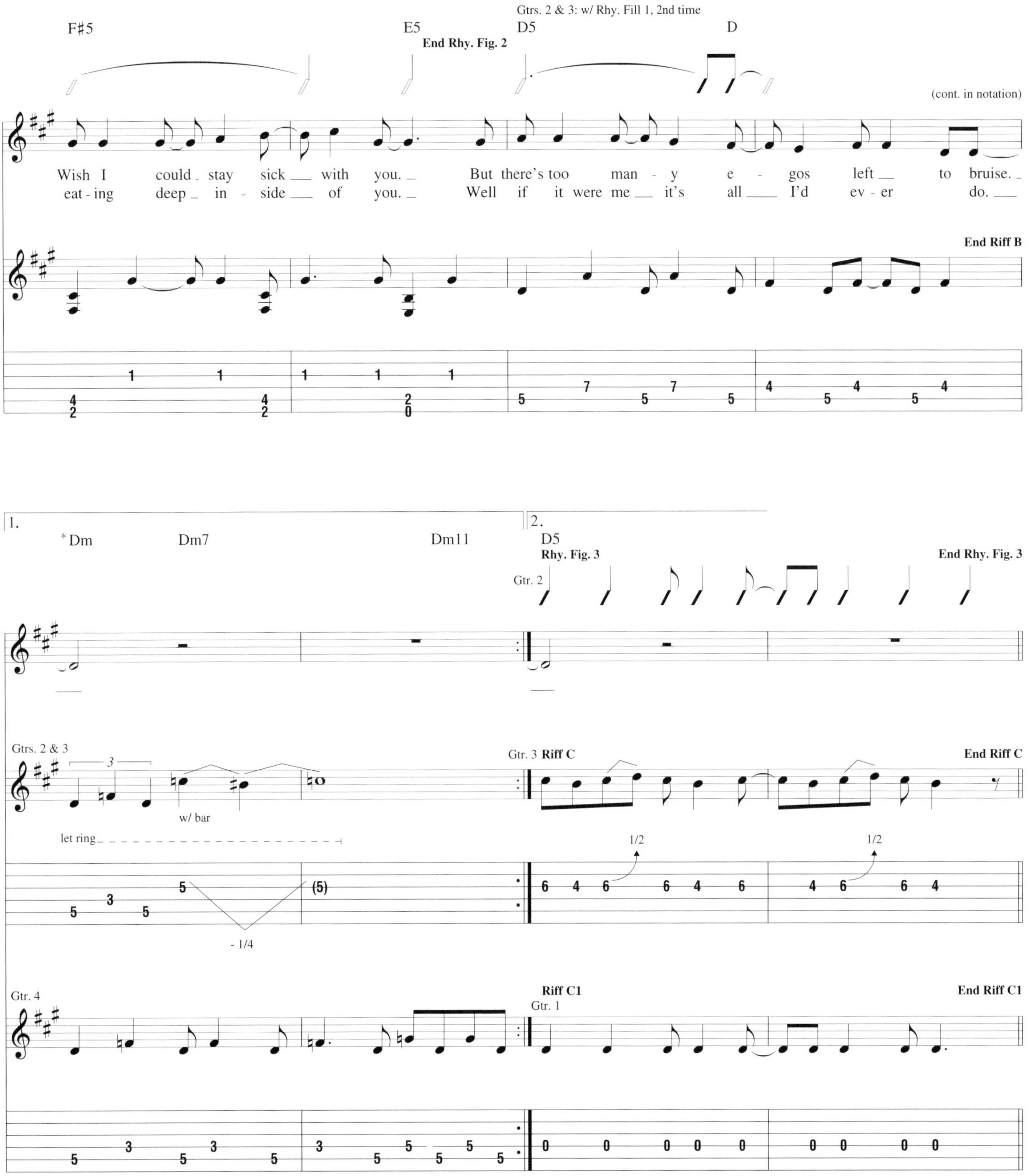

1.
*Dm Dm7 Dm11

2.
D5
Rhy. Fig. 3
End Rhy. Fig. 3
Gtr. 2

Gtrs. 2 & 3
Gtr. 3 Riff C
End Riff C
w/ bar
let ring
1/2
1/2
- 1/4

Gtr. 4
Riff C1
Gtr. 1
End Riff C1

* Chord symbols reflect combined tonality.

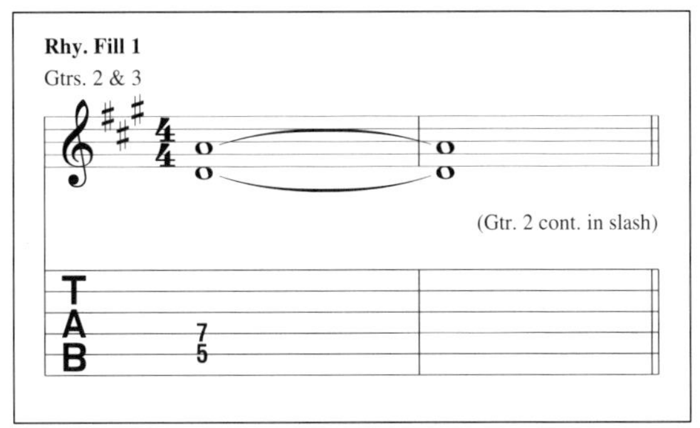

Interlude

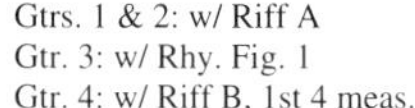
Gtrs. 1 & 2: w/ Riff A
Gtr. 3: w/ Rhy. Fig. 1
Gtr. 4: w/ Riff B, 1st 4 meas.

Gtr. 4: w/ Riff B, 1st 3 meas.

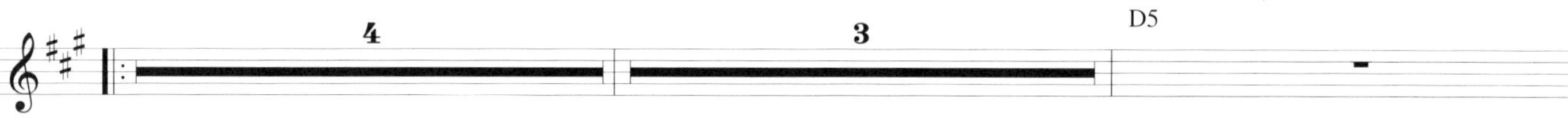
4
3
Gtr. 4: w/ Riff B, 5th meas.
D5

Verse
Gtr. 1: w/ Fill 1, simile
Gtrs. 2 & 3: w/ Rhy. Fig. 2
Gtr. 4: w/ Riff B
A5
E5
F#5
E5
3. Steal me now __ and for - ev - er. I'll steal some - thing good __ for you. __ The
4. Send me out __ on a teth - er. Swing it 'round _ I'll spin __ your noose. . You

Gtrs. 2 & 3: w/ Rhy. Fill 1, simile
D5
Gtr. 2: w/ Rhy. Fig. 3
Gtrs. 3 & 4: w/ Riffs C & C1
crim - i - nal __ in me __ is no __ one new. __
let it down _ I'll hang __ a - round __ with you. __

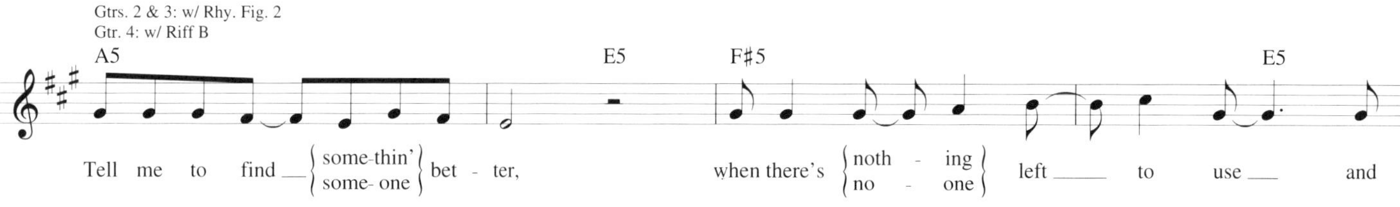
Gtrs. 2 & 3: w/ Rhy. Fig. 2
Gtr. 4: w/ Riff B
A5
E5
F#5
E5
Tell me to find __ { some-thin' / some- one } bet - ter, when there's { noth - ing / no - one } left __ to use __ and

Gtrs. 2 & 3: w/ Rhy. Fill 1, simile
D5
Gtr. 2: w/ Rhy. Fig. 3, simile
Gtrs. 3 & 4: w/ Riffs C & C1
ev - 'ry - thing __ starts go - ing down _ on you. __
ev - 'ry - one __ keeps go - ing down. __

Chorus
A5
A+(no3rd)
I'm the gen - er - a - tor fir - ing when - ev - er you quit. __
Gtrs. 2 & 3
Rhy. Fig. 4
simile on repeats

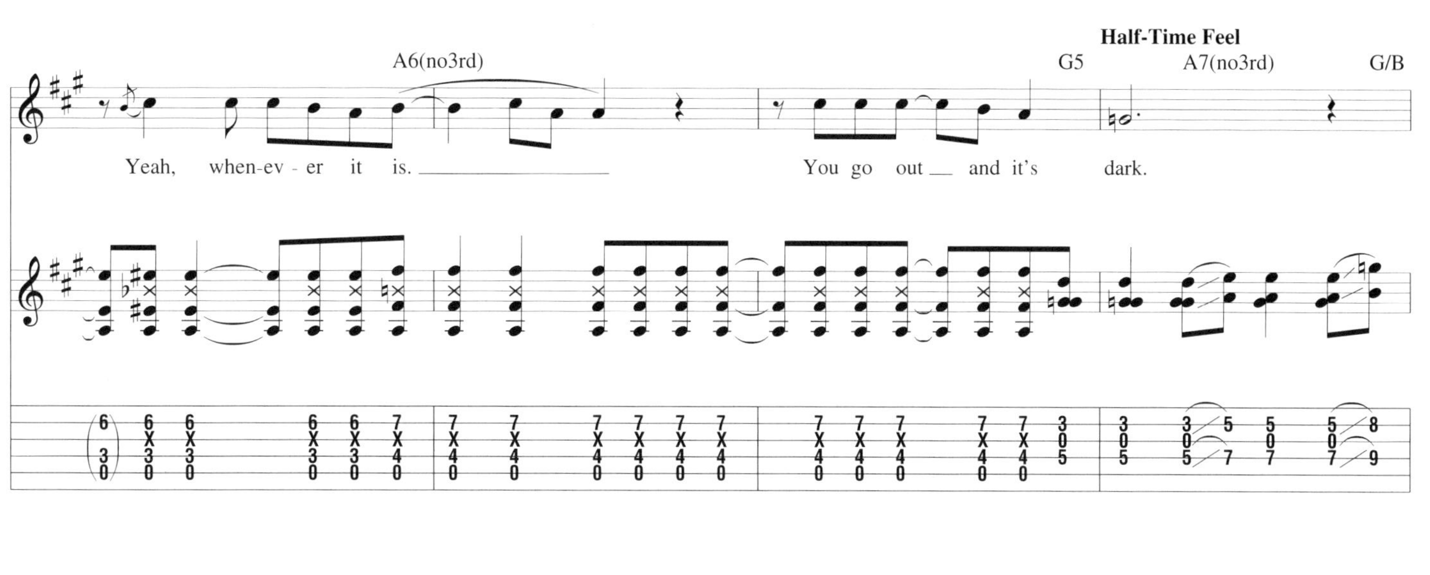

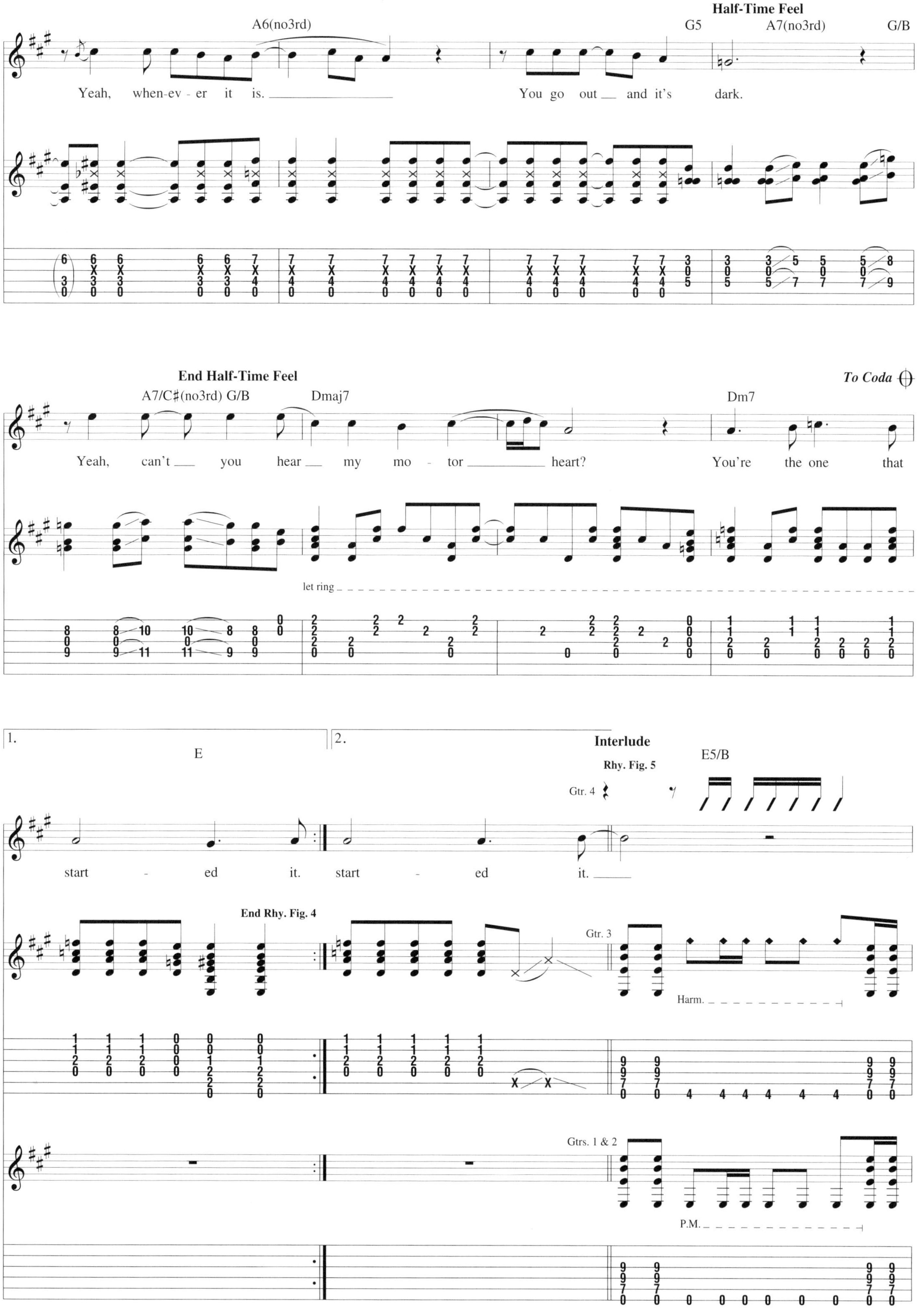

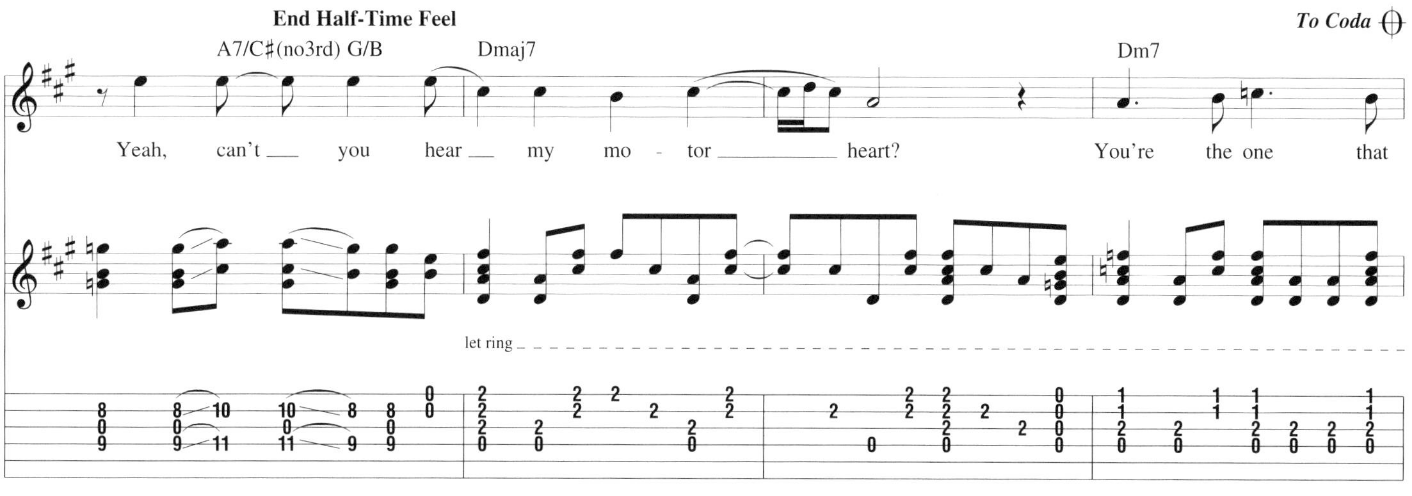

Half-Time Feel
A6(no3rd)
G5
A7(no3rd)
G/B
Yeah, when-ev - er it is.
You go out and it's dark.
End Half-Time Feel
To Coda
A7/C♯(no3rd) G/B
Dmaj7
Dm7
Yeah, can't you hear my mo - tor heart?
You're the one that
let ring
1.
2.
Interlude
E
E5/B
Rhy. Fig. 5
Gtr. 4
start - ed it. start - ed it.
End Rhy. Fig. 4
Gtr. 3
Harm.
Gtrs. 1 & 2
P.M.

End Rhy. Fig. 5
Harm.
P.M.
1., 2., 3.
4.
D.S. al Coda
* Gtrs. 1, 2 & 3
Gtr. 4: w/ Rhy. Fig. 5, 2 times, simile
E5
* composite arrangement
Coda
Chorus
Gtrs. 2 & 3: w/ Rhy. Fig. 4, last meas.
Gtrs. 2 & 3: w/ Rhy. Fig. 4, simile
Dm7
E
A5
start - ed it.
I'm the gen - er - a - tor, I'm the gen - er - a - tor. I'm
A+(no3rd)
A6(no3rd)
the gen - er - a - tor, I'm the gen - er - a - tor. I'm the gen - er - a - tor, I'm
Half-Time Feel
End Half-Time Feel
G5
A7(no3rd)
G/B
A7/C♯(no3rd) G/B
the gen - er - a - tor you're on.
Yeah, can't you hear
Dmaj7
Dm7
E
my mo - tor heart? You're the one that start - ed it.
Outro
Gtrs. 1 & 2
Gtr. 3: w/ Rhy. Fig. 1, 1st 2 meas., 2 times, simile
A5
E5
A5
E5
Gtrs. 1, 2 & 3
A5

Aurora

Words and Music by Dave Grohl, Nate Mendel and Taylor Hawkins

*composite arrangement

mp
mf
(cont. in notation)
We will al - ways have that chance, we can do this one more time.
Chorus
Gtr. 2 tacet
A Amaj7 Amaj9 A♭sus2 A5 A Amaj7
Hell yeah, I re-mem-ber Au-ro - ra. Hell yeah,
Gtr. 5 (dist.)
mp
Gtrs. 3 & 4
f
simile on repeat
Amaj9 A6sus2 A5 Dmaj#11/A D/A Dmaj#11/A
I re-mem-ber Au-ro - ra, all this time.
let ring

D5/A D6/A D5/A D/A A Amaj7

Hell yeah,

Gtr. 5 tacet

Amaj9 A6sus2 A5 N.C.(D) (A)

I re - mem - ber Au - ro - ra. Take me now.

Rhy. Fig. 1

(D)
(A)
(D)
We could spin the sun a - round, and the stars
Gtrs. 3 & 4
(A)
F5
G5
N.C.(A)
will all come out then we'll turn and come back down.
To Coda
F5
G5
Gtr. 1: w/ Riff A, 1 3/4 times, simile
A5
Turn and come back down.
End Rhy. Fig. 1
2. You be - lieve

Verse

Asus2 Amaj7 A

there some - where else

Gtr. 3 *mp* Gtr. 5 *p* Gtr. 3 *divisi*

Gtr. 2

Asus2 A

where it's eas - i - er than this.

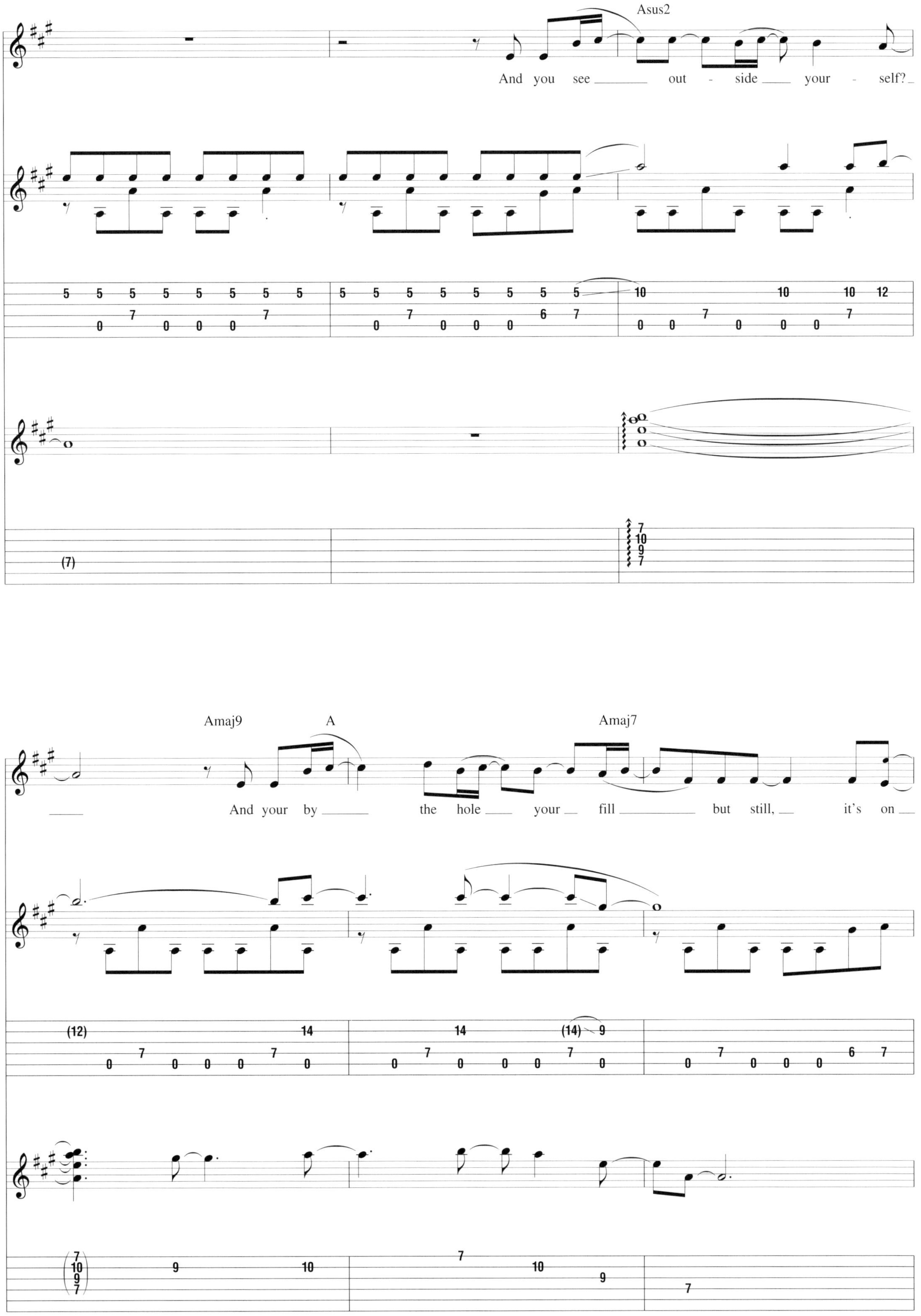

Asus2

And you see out - side your - self?

Amaj9 A Amaj7

And your by the hole your fill but still, it's on

D.S. al Coda

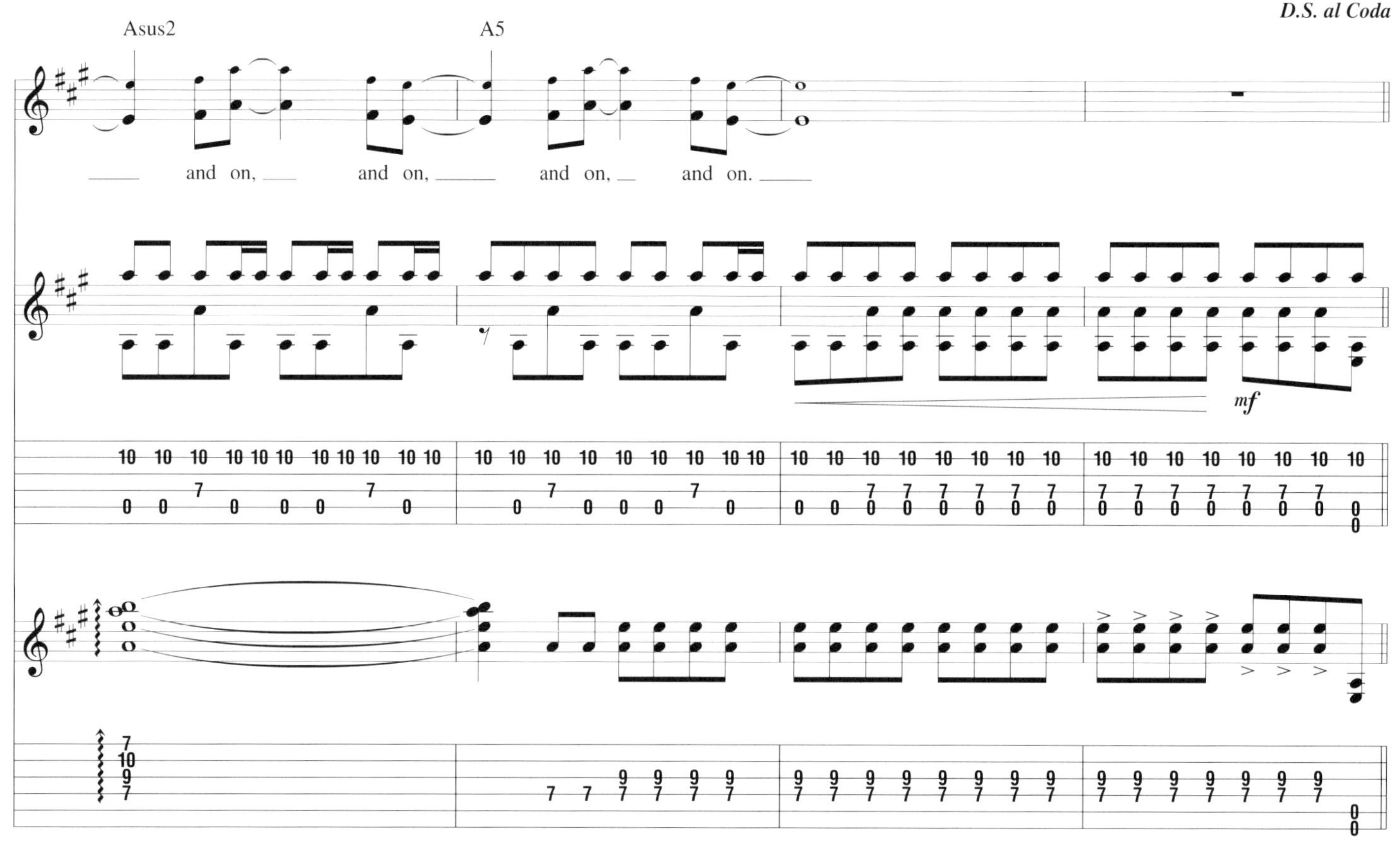

Asus2
A5
and on, and on, and on, and on.
mf

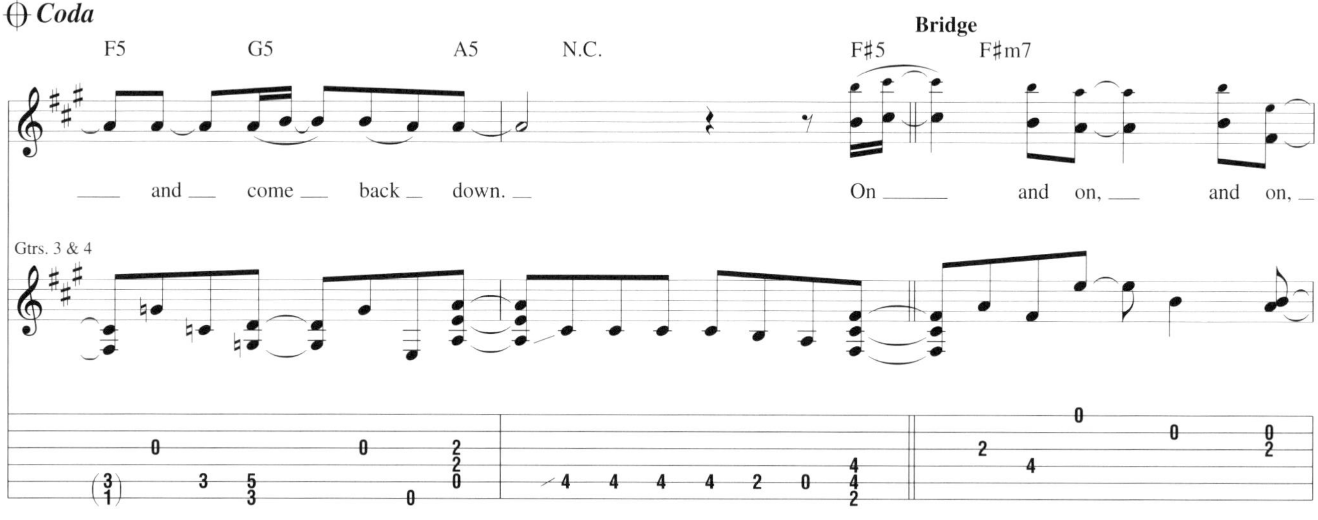

Coda
Bridge
F5
G5
A5
N.C.
F♯5
F♯m7
and come back down.
On and on, and on,
Gtrs. 3 & 4

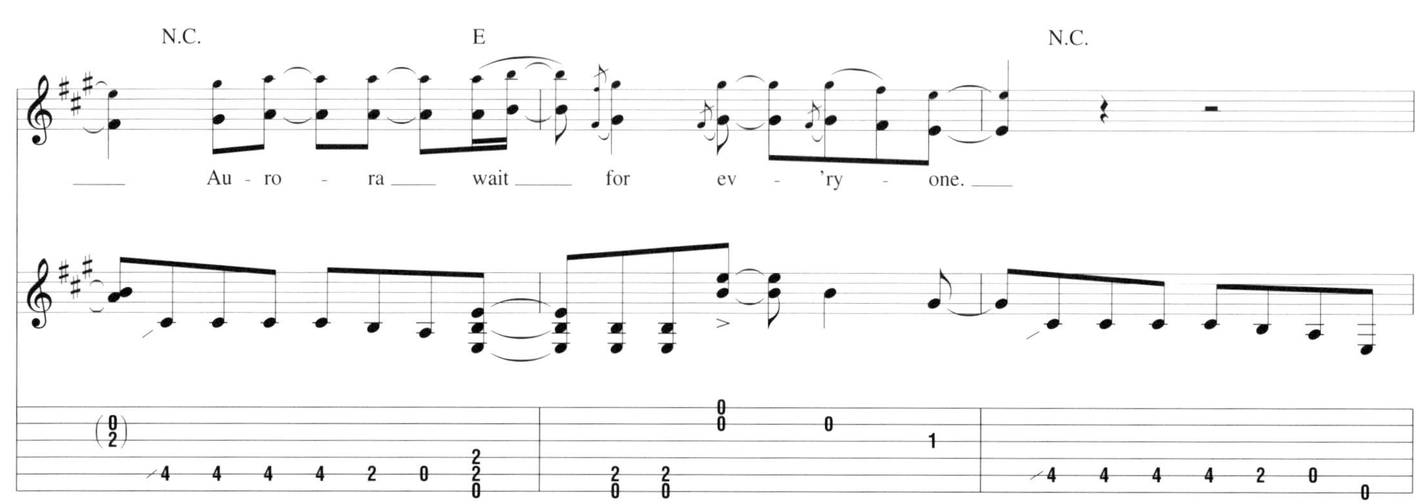

N.C.
E
N.C.
Au - ro - ra wait for ev - 'ry - one.

F5 G5 A5 N.C. F♯5 F♯m7 N.C. E
Wait till the last fal-ling star. On and on, and on, Au-ro-ra wait
N.C. F5 G5 A5 N.C.(D)
for ev-'ry-one. Wait till the last fal-ling star. Take
Chorus
Gtrs. 3 & 4: w/ Rhy. Fig. 1, simile
N.C.(D) (A) (D) (A) (D)
me now. we can spin the sun a-round. And the stars
(A) F5 G5 A F5
will all come out, then we'll turn and come back down. Turn
G5 N.C.(A7) F5 G5 N.C.(A7)
and come back down. Turn and come back down.
Gtrs. 3 & 4

Interlude
Gtr. 1: w/ Riff A, 2 1/2 times, simile
F5
G5
A5
Turn and come back down.
Gtrs. 3 & 4 tacet
Asus2
Outro
Gtr. 1: w/ Riff A, 3 times, simile
A5
Asus2
On and on, and on,
Gtr. 2
Gtr. 5: w/ Fill 1
A5
Amaj7
Asus2
and on, and on, and on, and on, and on, and on, and on, and on,
Fill 1
Gtr. 3
play 8 times
mp
* vol. swell

A
5 open
Gtr. 1: w/ Rhy. Fill 1
Gtr. 3
mp
(cont. in notation)
and on, and on, and on, and on, and on, and on, and on, and on,
Gtr. 2
Gtr. 4
Gtr. 2 divisi
Gtr. 2 tacet
A
Asus2
A
Asus2
and on.
Gtrs. 3 & 4
Rhy. Fig. 2
End Rhy. Fig. 2
f
Gtrs. 3 & 4: w/ Rhy. Fig. 2, simile
Gtr. 1: w/ Riff A, 8 times, simile
* A
Gtr. 2
Gtrs. 3 & 4 divisi
Rhy. Fig. 3
End Rhy. Fig. 3
* Chord symbols reflect overall tonality.

Rhy. Fill 1
Gtr. 1
mp
T
A
B

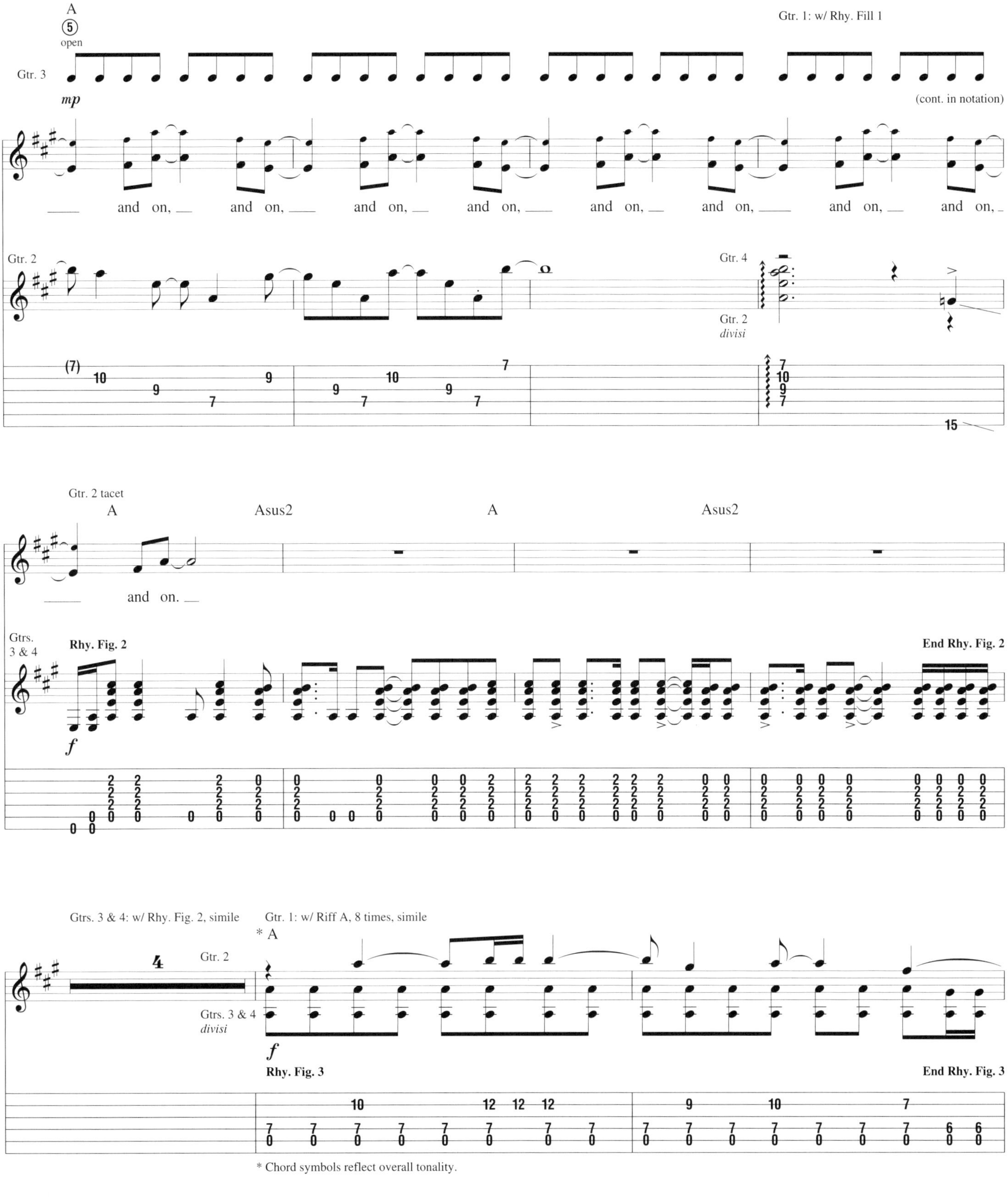

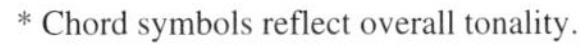

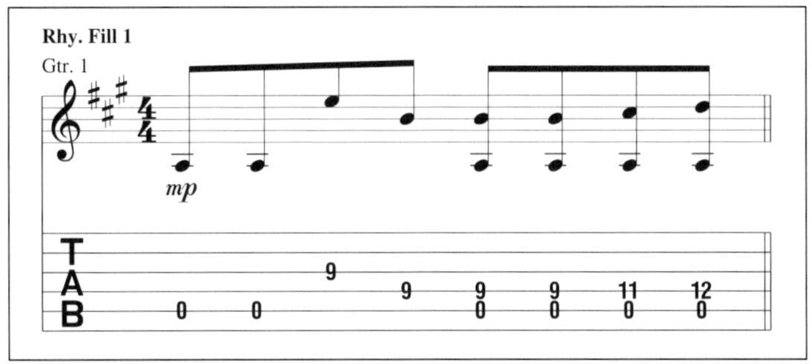

Gtr. 2
Gtrs. 3 & 4: w/ Rhy. Fig. 3, 3 times, simile

Gtr. 2: w/ Fill 2
N.C.(A)
Gtr. 1
Gtrs. 3 & 4
* w/ echo repeats, 2nd time

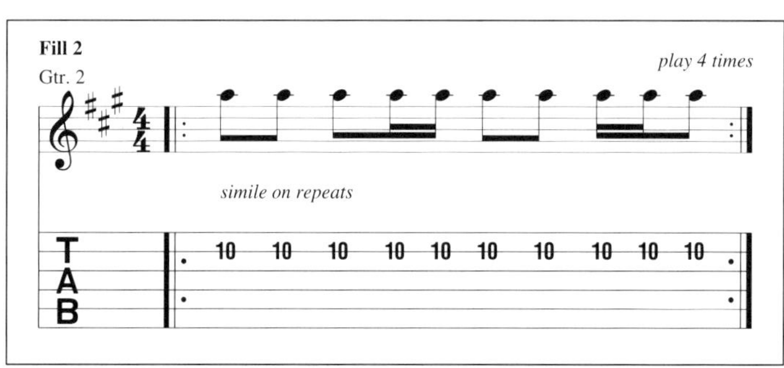
Fill 2
Gtr. 2
play 4 times
simile on repeats

Live-In Skin

Words and Music by Dave Grohl, Nate Mendel and Taylor Hawkins

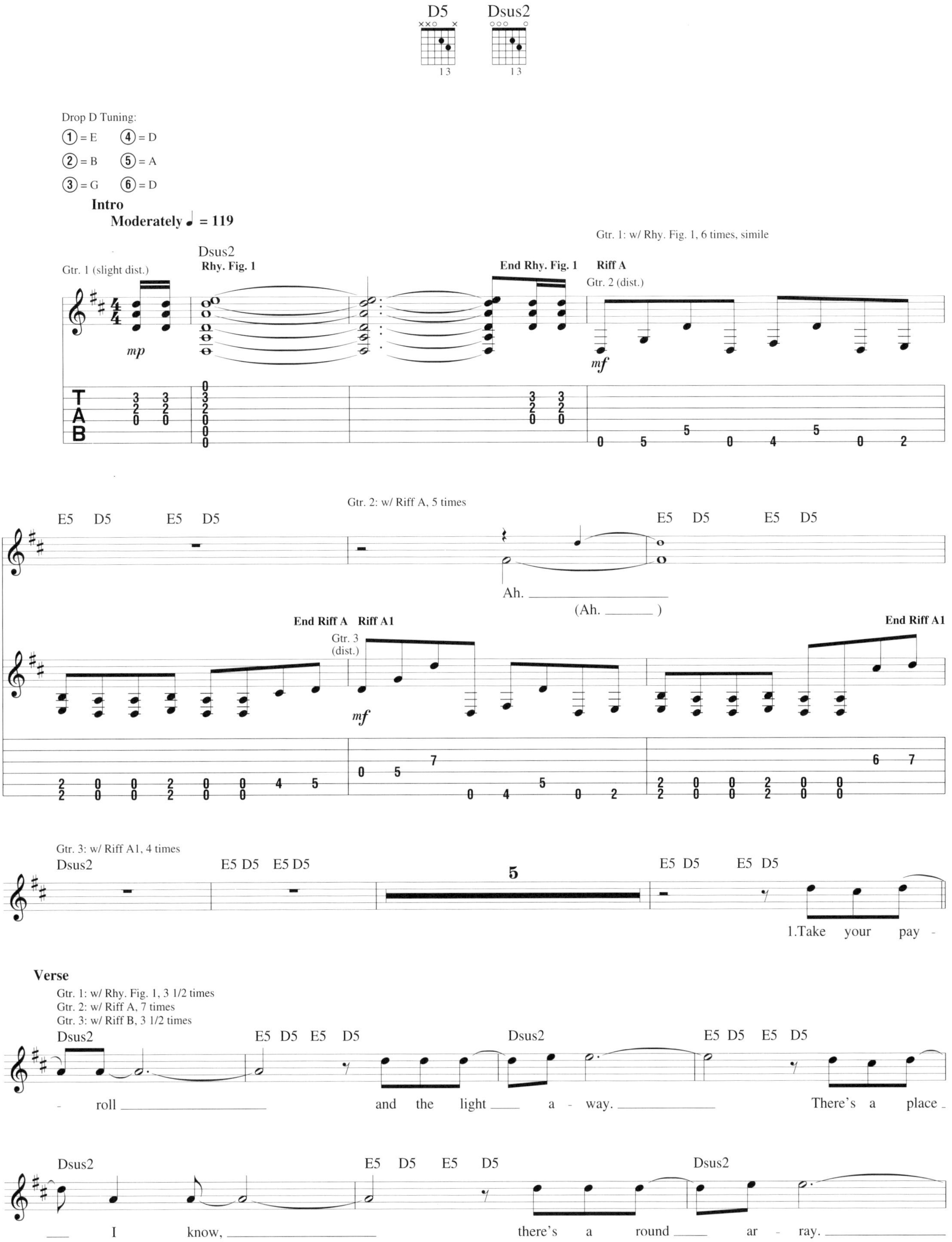

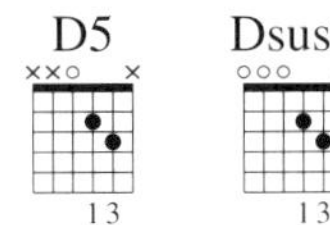

Drop D Tuning:
① = E ④ = D
② = B ⑤ = A
③ = G ⑥ = D

Intro
Moderately ♩ = 119

Gtr. 1: w/ Rhy. Fig. 1, 6 times, simile
Dsus2
Gtr. 1 (slight dist.) Rhy. Fig. 1 End Rhy. Fig. 1 Riff A
Gtr. 2 (dist.)
mp *mf*

E5 D5 E5 D5 Gtr. 2: w/ Riff A, 5 times E5 D5 E5 D5

Ah. (Ah.)

End Riff A Riff A1 End Riff A1
Gtr. 3 (dist.)
mf

Gtr. 3: w/ Riff A1, 4 times
Dsus2 E5 D5 E5 D5 5 E5 D5 E5 D5

1.Take your pay -

Verse
Gtr. 1: w/ Rhy. Fig. 1, 3 1/2 times
Gtr. 2: w/ Riff A, 7 times
Gtr. 3: w/ Riff B, 3 1/2 times
Dsus2 E5 D5 E5 D5 Dsus2 E5 D5 E5 D5

- roll and the light a - way. There's a place

Dsus2 E5 D5 E5 D5 Dsus2

I know, there's a round ar - ray.

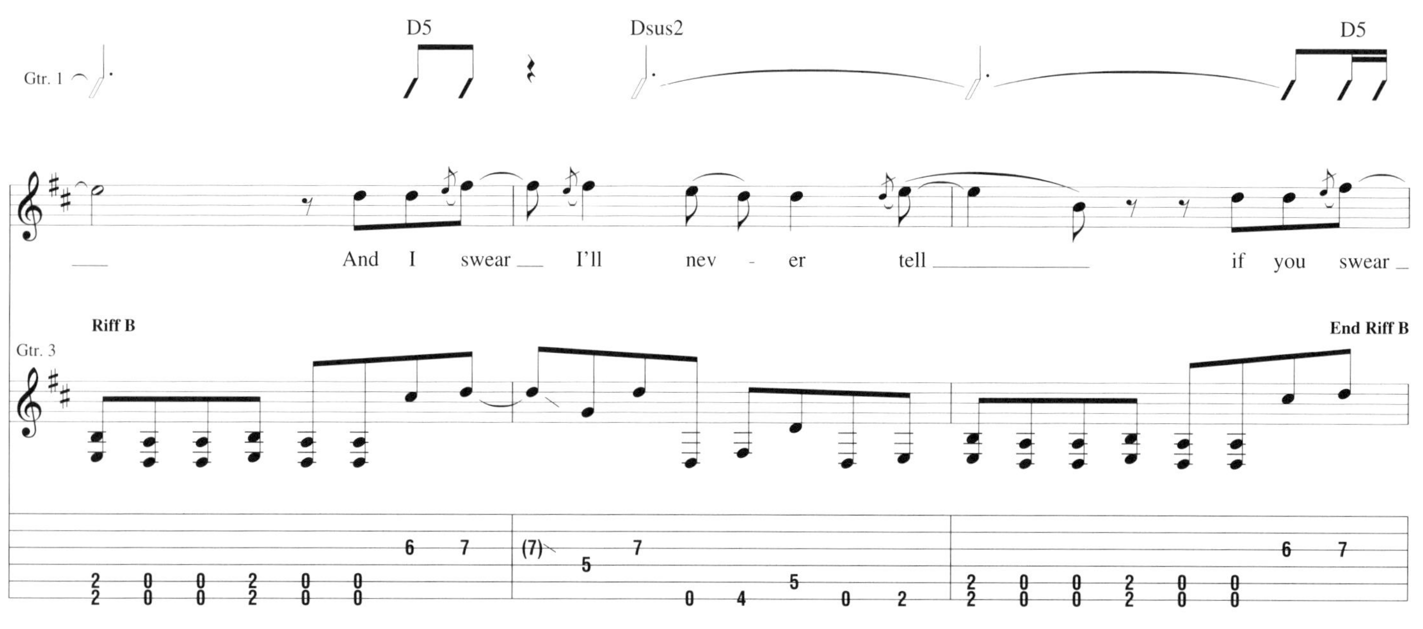

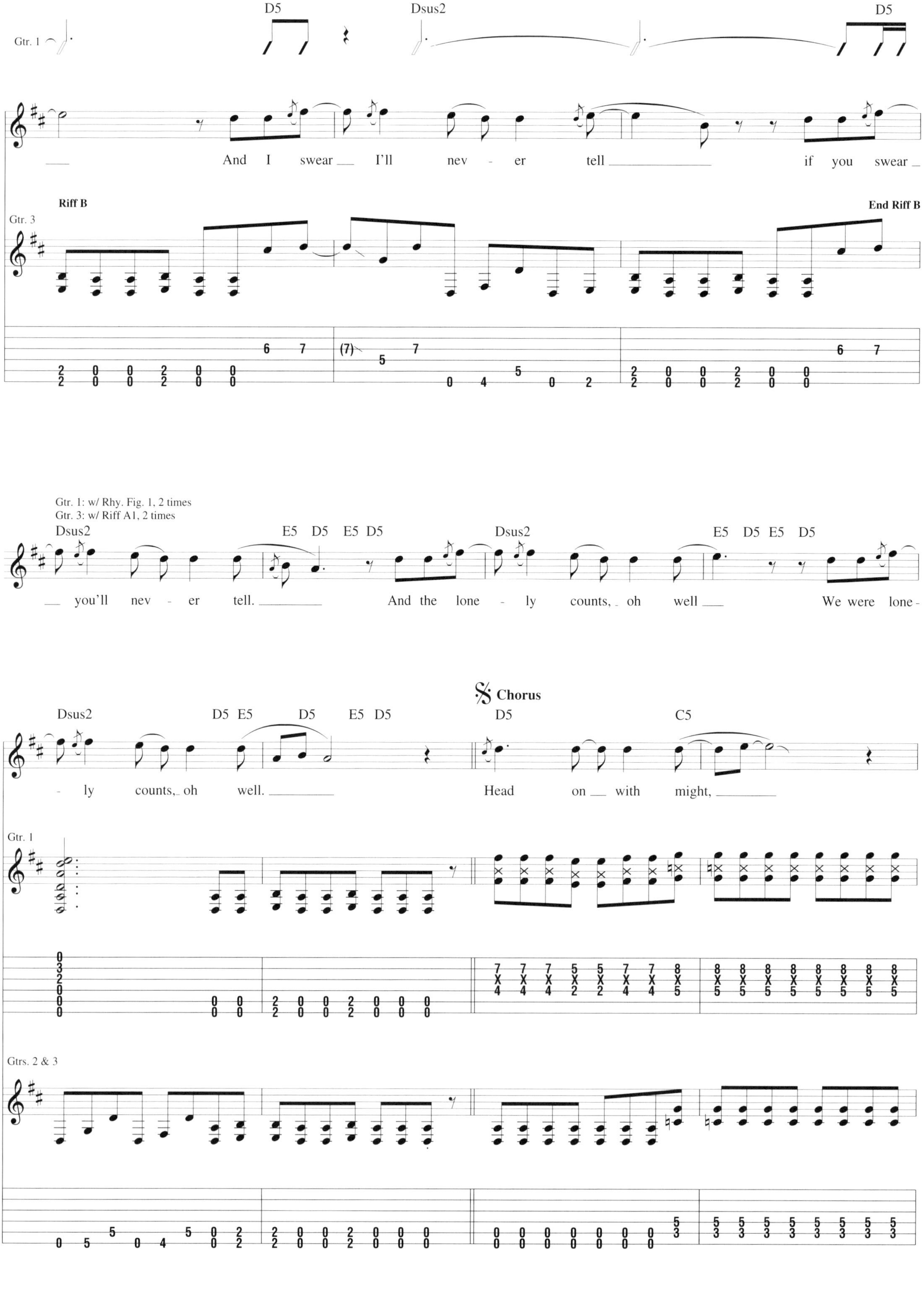

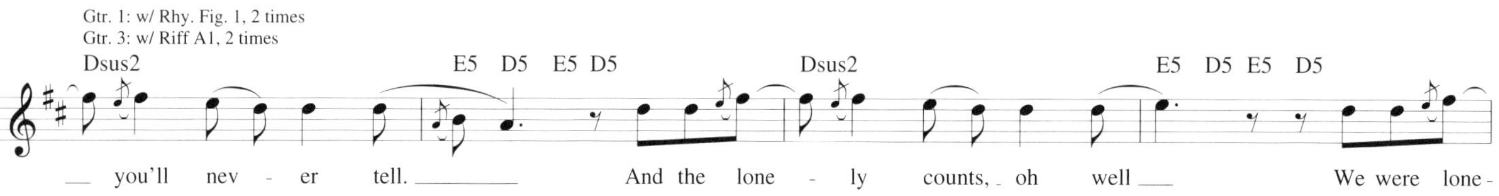

Chorus

Dsus2 D5 E5 D5 E5 D5 D5 C5

- ly counts, oh well. Head on with might,

Gtr. 1

Gtrs. 2 & 3

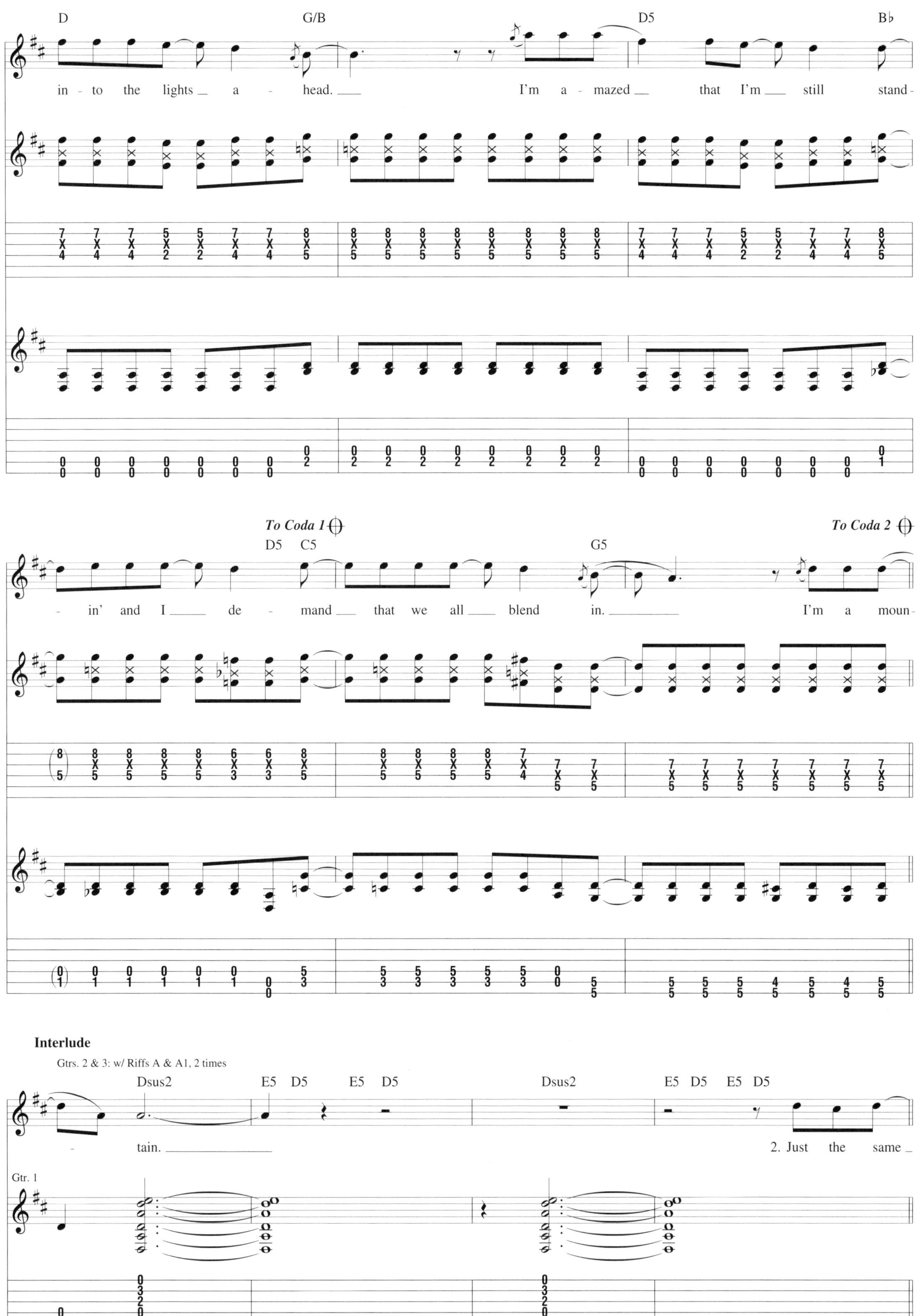
D
G/B
D5
B♭
in - to the lights a - head. I'm a - mazed that I'm still stand -
To Coda 1
To Coda 2
D5 C5
G5
- in' and I de - mand that we all blend in. I'm a moun -
Interlude
Gtrs. 2 & 3: w/ Riffs A & A1, 2 times
Dsus2
E5 D5 E5 D5
Dsus2
E5 D5 E5 D5
- tain. 2. Just the same
Gtr. 1

Verse
Gtr. 2: w/ Riff A, 7 times
Gtr. 3: w/ Riff A1, 3 1/2 times
D5 E5 D5 E5 D5 Dsus2 E5 D5 E5 D5
though, clear the storm a - way. From the sea
Rhy. Fig. 2
End Rhy. Fig. 2
Dsus2 E5 D5 E5 D5 Dsus2
Gtr. 3: w/ Riff B
E5 D5 E5 D5
floor, met - a - mor - phi - sis. And I can't
Gtr. 1: w/ Rhy. Fig. 2, 3 times
Dsus2 E5 D5 E5 D5
Gtr. 3: w/ Riff A1, 2 times
Dsus2
change back for you. I will not change back for you.
E5 D5 E5 D5 Dsus2 E5 D5 E5 D5
I must live in skin that's new. I'm a liv -
D.S. al Coda 1
Dsus2 E5 D5 E5 D5
- in' skin that's new.
Gtr. 1
Gtrs. 2 & 3
Coda 1
D.S. al Coda 2
C5 G5
that we all blend in.

Coda 2

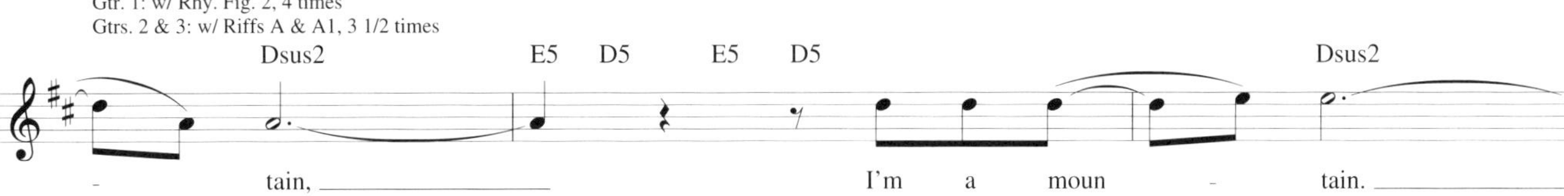
Gtr. 1: w/ Rhy. Fig. 2, 4 times
Gtrs. 2 & 3: w/ Riffs A & A1, 3 1/2 times
Dsus2 E5 D5 E5 D5 Dsus2
- tain, I'm a moun - tain.

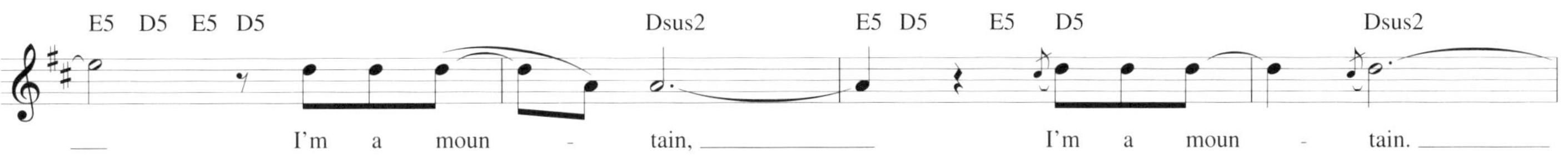
E5 D5 E5 D5 Dsus2 E5 D5 E5 D5 Dsus2
I'm a moun - tain, I'm a moun - tain.

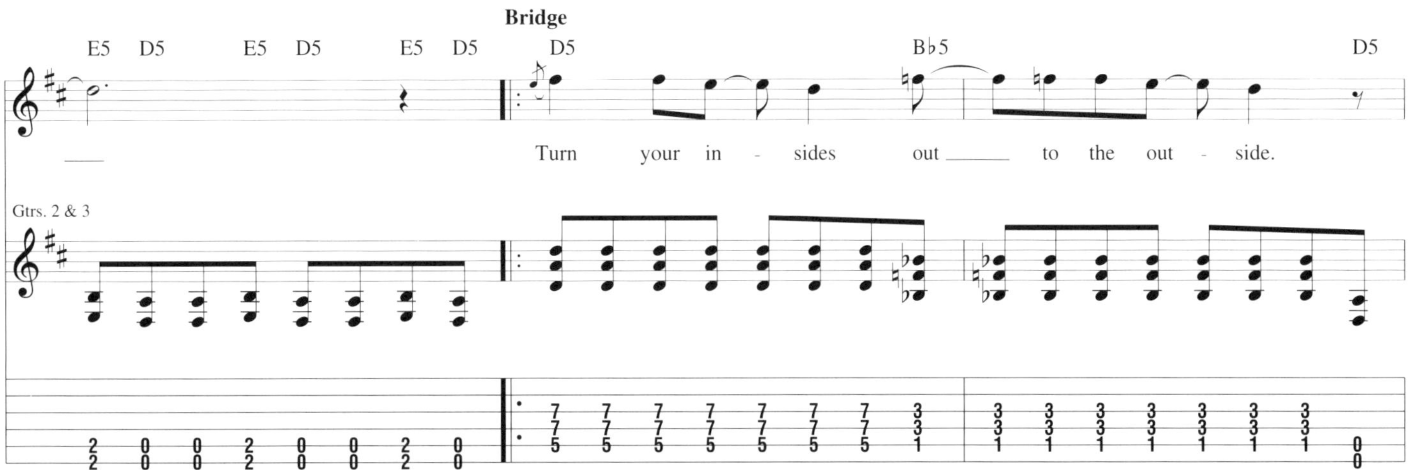
Bridge
E5 D5 E5 D5 E5 D5 D5 B♭5 D5
Turn your in - sides out to the out - side.
Gtrs. 2 & 3

B♭5 D5 B♭5
Turn the out - side in - to the in - side. Trade your out - side in for the in - side.

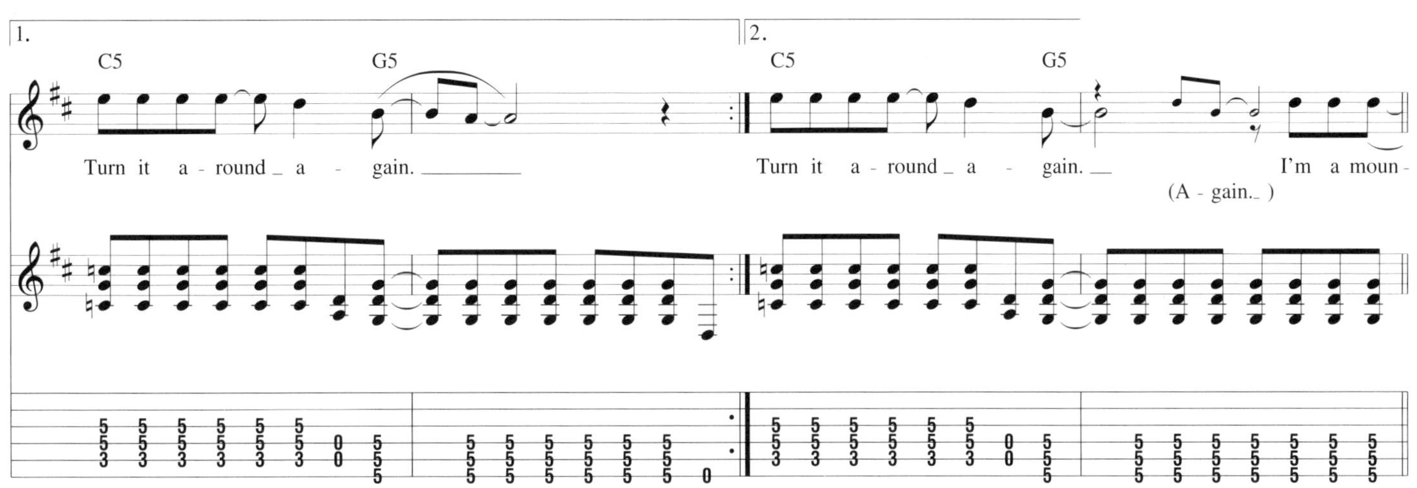
1. 2.
C5 G5 C5 G5
Turn it a - round a - gain. Turn it a - round a - gain. I'm a moun -
(A - gain.)

Outro
Gtr. 1: w/ Rhy. Fig. 2, 8 times
Gtrs. 2 & 3: w/ Riffs A & A1, 3 1/2 times
Dsus2 E5 D5 E5 D5 Dsus2 E5 D5 E5 D5
- tain, I'm a moun - tain. I'm a moun -
Dsus2 E5 D5 E5 D5 Dsus2
- tain, I'm a moun - tain.
(Moun - tain. Moun - tain.
E5 D5 E5 D5 Dsus2 E5 D5 E5 D5
And I can't change back for you. No, I can't
)
Gtr. 3
Riff C1
End Riff C1
Gtr. 2
Riff C
End Riff C
Gtrs. 2 & 3: w/ Riffs C & C1, 2 times
Dsus2 E5 D5 E5 D5 Dsus2 E5 D5 E5 D5
change back for you. I'm a moun - tain.
Gtr. 3
Dsus2 E5 D5 E5 D5
Gtr. 2

Next Year

Words and Music by Dave Grohl, Nate Mendel and Taylor Hawkins

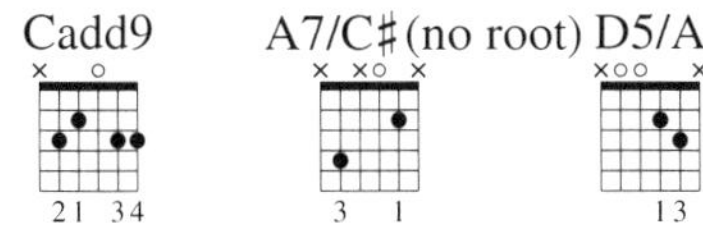

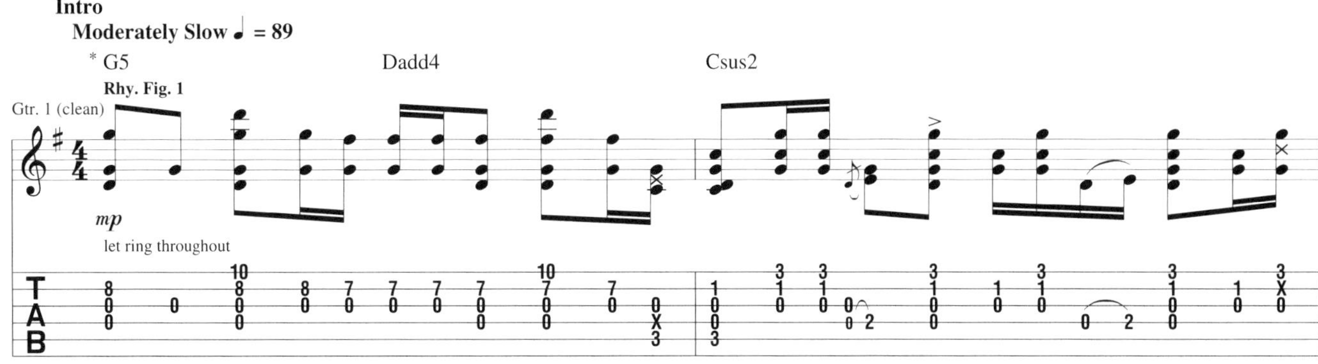

* Chord symbols reflect overall tonality.

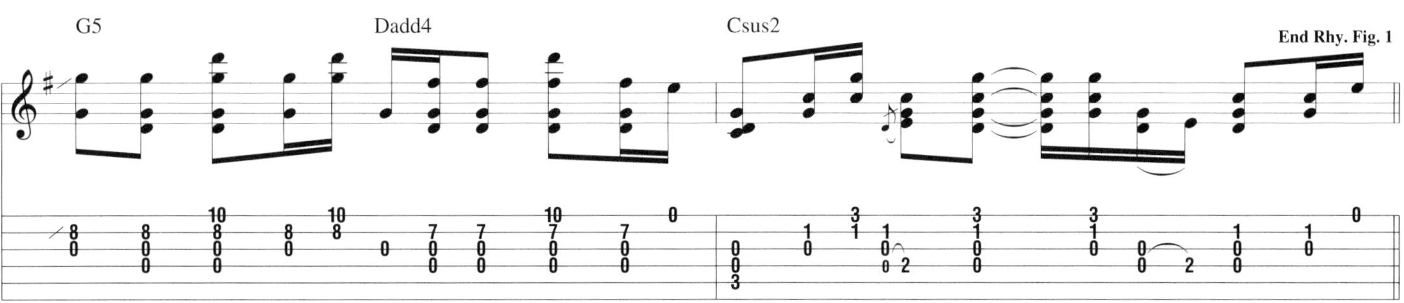

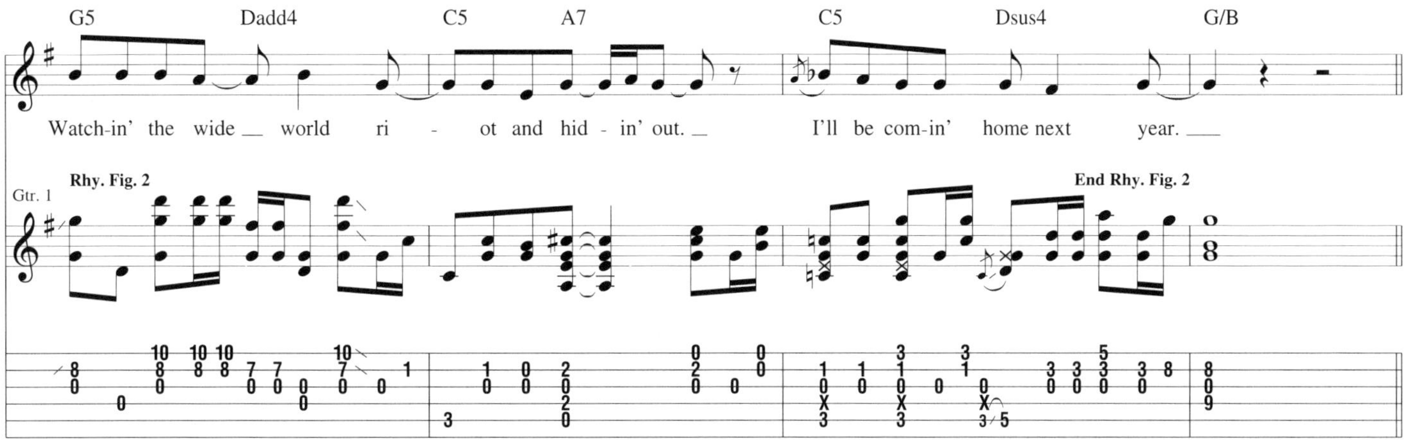

Interlude
* Gtrs. 1 & 2: w/ Rhy. Fig. 1, simile
** G5
Dadd4
Cadd9
Rhy. Fig. 3
Gtr. 3 (slight dist.)
mf
let ring throughout
* Gtr. 2 (slight dist.)
** Chord symbols reflect overall tonality.
End Rhy. Fig. 3
Verse
Gtrs. 1 & 2: w/ Rhy. Fig. 1, simile
Gtr. 3: w/ Rhy. Fig. 3, simile
2. In - to the sun we climb.
4. I'm in the sky to - night.
Climb and our wings will burn white.
There I can keep by your side.
Gtrs. 1 & 2: w/ Rhy. Fig. 2, simile
A7
Ev - 'ry - one's strapped in tight, we'll ride it out.
Watch - in' the whole world wide and 'round and 'round.
Rhy. Fig. 4
Gtr. 3
simile on repeat
I'll be com - in' home next year.
Rhy. Fill 1
Gtr. 1
End Rhy. Fill 1
Gtrs. 2 & 3
End Rhy. Fig. 4

Chorus

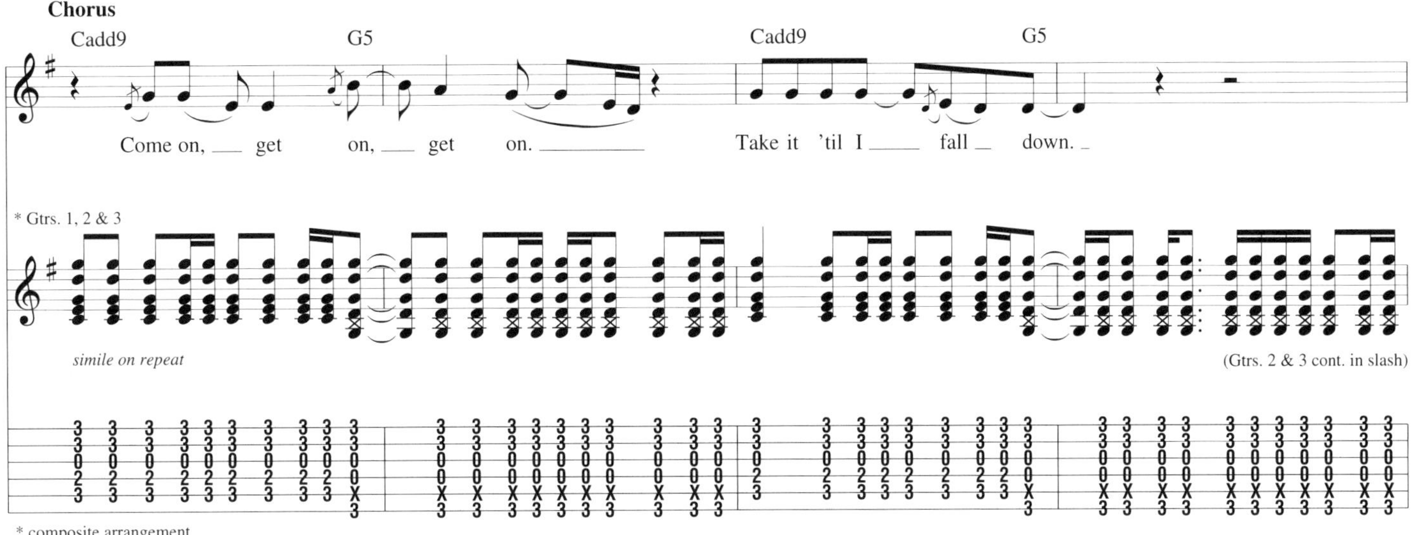

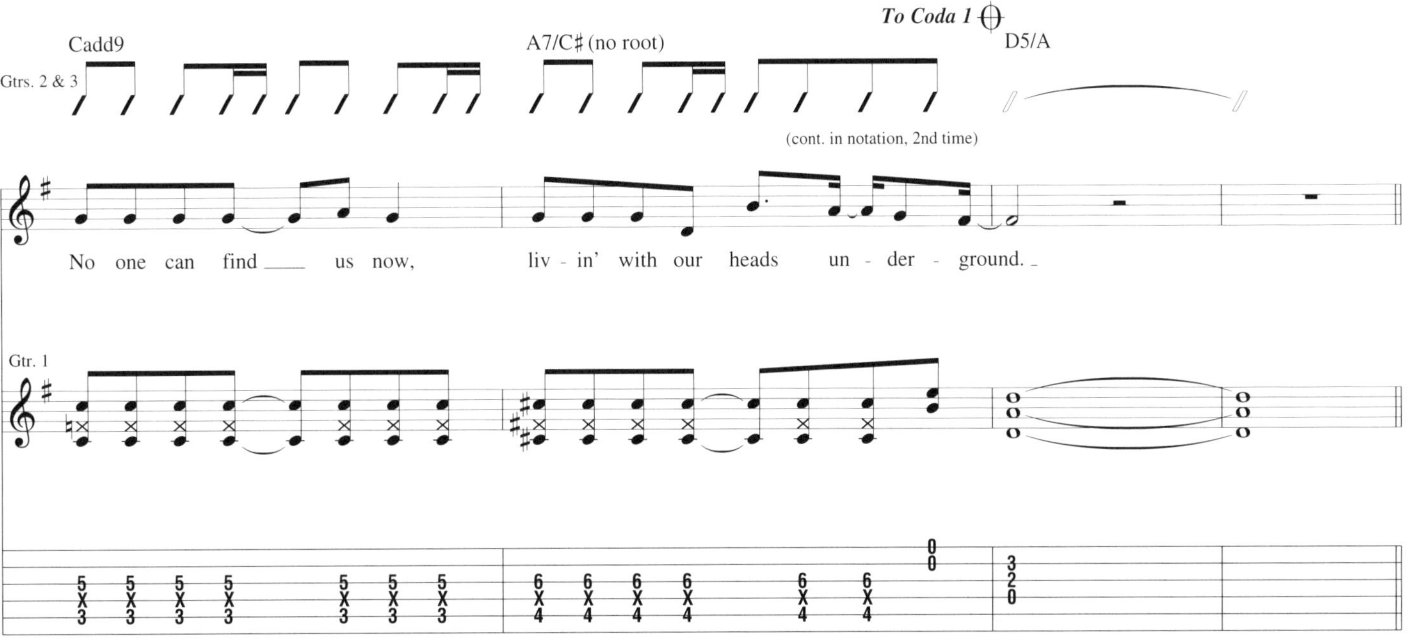

Verse

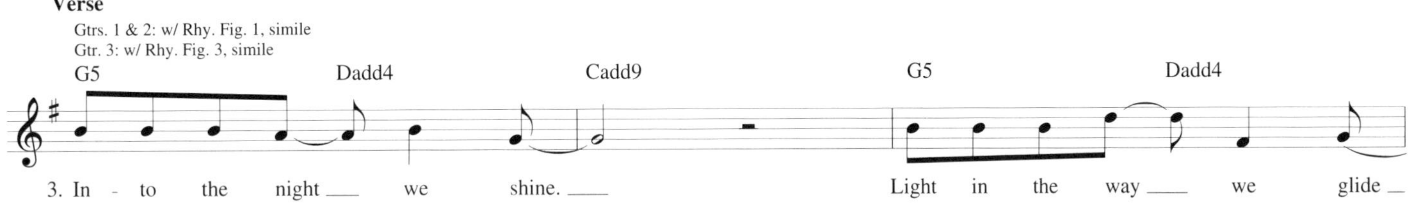

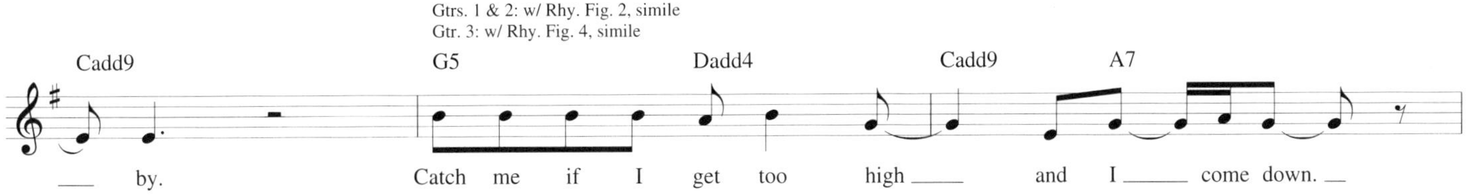

D.S. al Coda 1
Gtr. 1: w/ Rhy. Fill 1
Gtr. 2: w/ Rhy. Fig. 4, last meas.
Cadd9
Dadd4
G5
I'll be com - ing home next year.

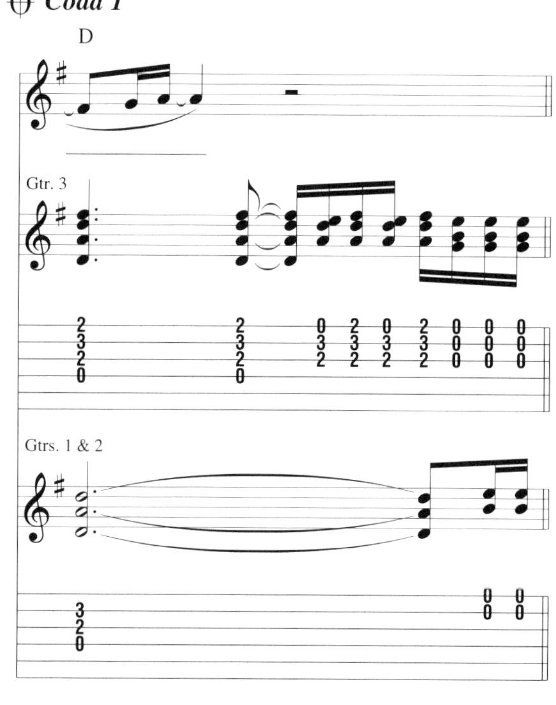
Coda 1
D
Gtr. 3
Gtrs. 1 & 2

Verse
Gtrs. 1 & 2: w/ Rhy. Fig. 1, simile
Gtr. 3: w/ Rhy. Fig. 3, simile
G5
Dadd4
Cadd9
5. I'll be com - in' home next year.
I'll be com - in' home next year.

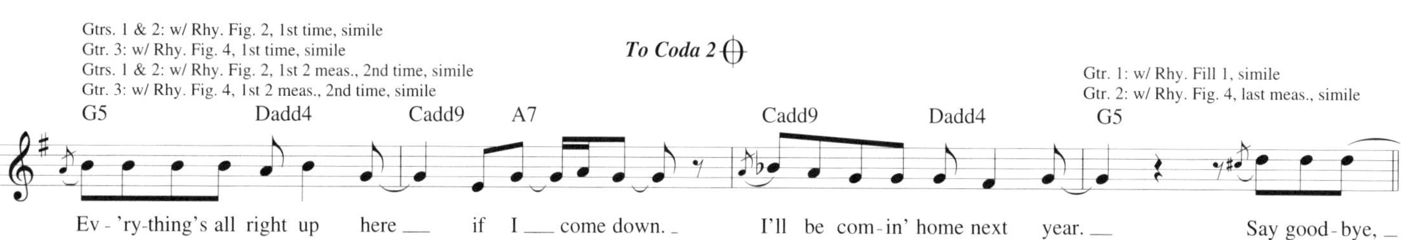
Gtrs. 1 & 2: w/ Rhy. Fig. 2, 1st time, simile
Gtr. 3: w/ Rhy. Fig. 4, 1st time, simile
Gtrs. 1 & 2: w/ Rhy. Fig. 2, 1st 2 meas., 2nd time, simile
Gtr. 3: w/ Rhy. Fig. 4, 1st 2 meas., 2nd time, simile
To Coda 2
Gtr. 1: w/ Rhy. Fill 1, simile
Gtr. 2: w/ Rhy. Fig. 4, last meas., simile
G5
Dadd4
Cadd9
A7
Cadd9
Dadd4
G5
Ev - 'ry-thing's all right up here if I come down.
I'll be com-in' home next year.
Say good - bye,

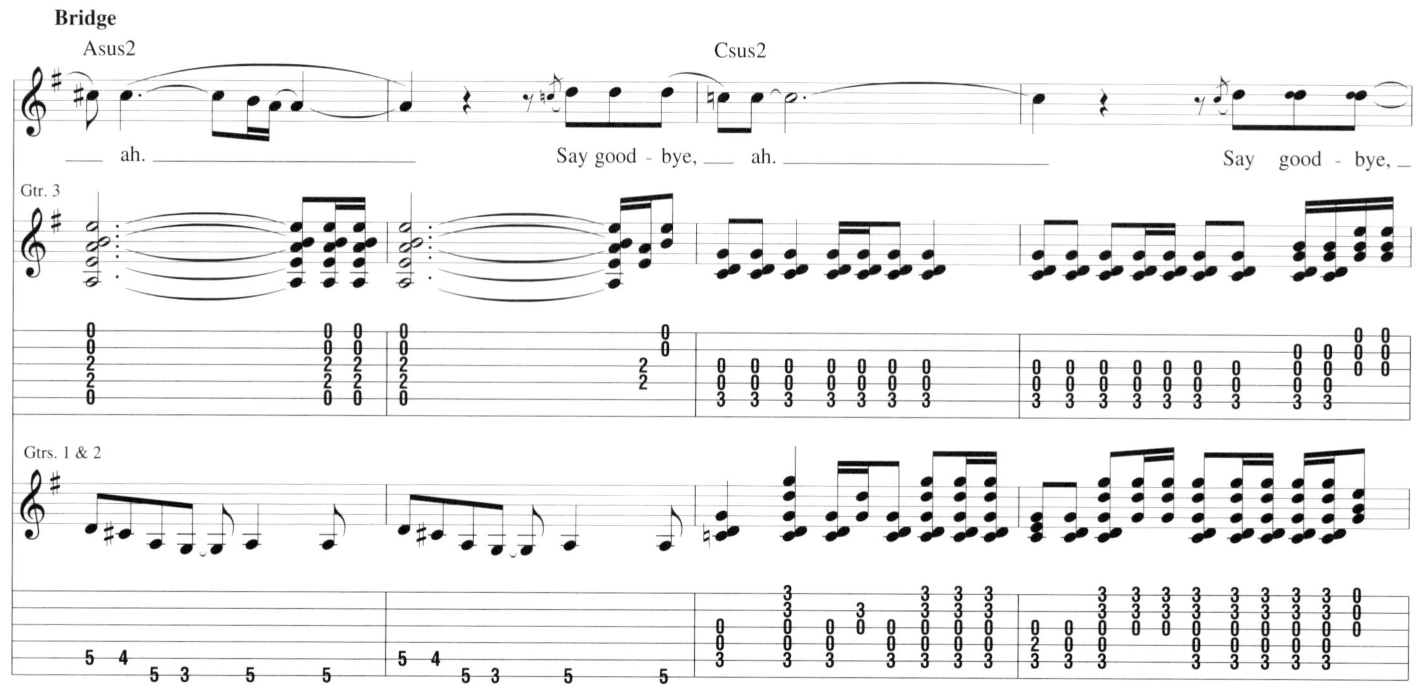
Bridge
Asus2
Csus2
ah.
Say good - bye, ah.
Say good - bye,
Gtr. 3
Gtrs. 1 & 2

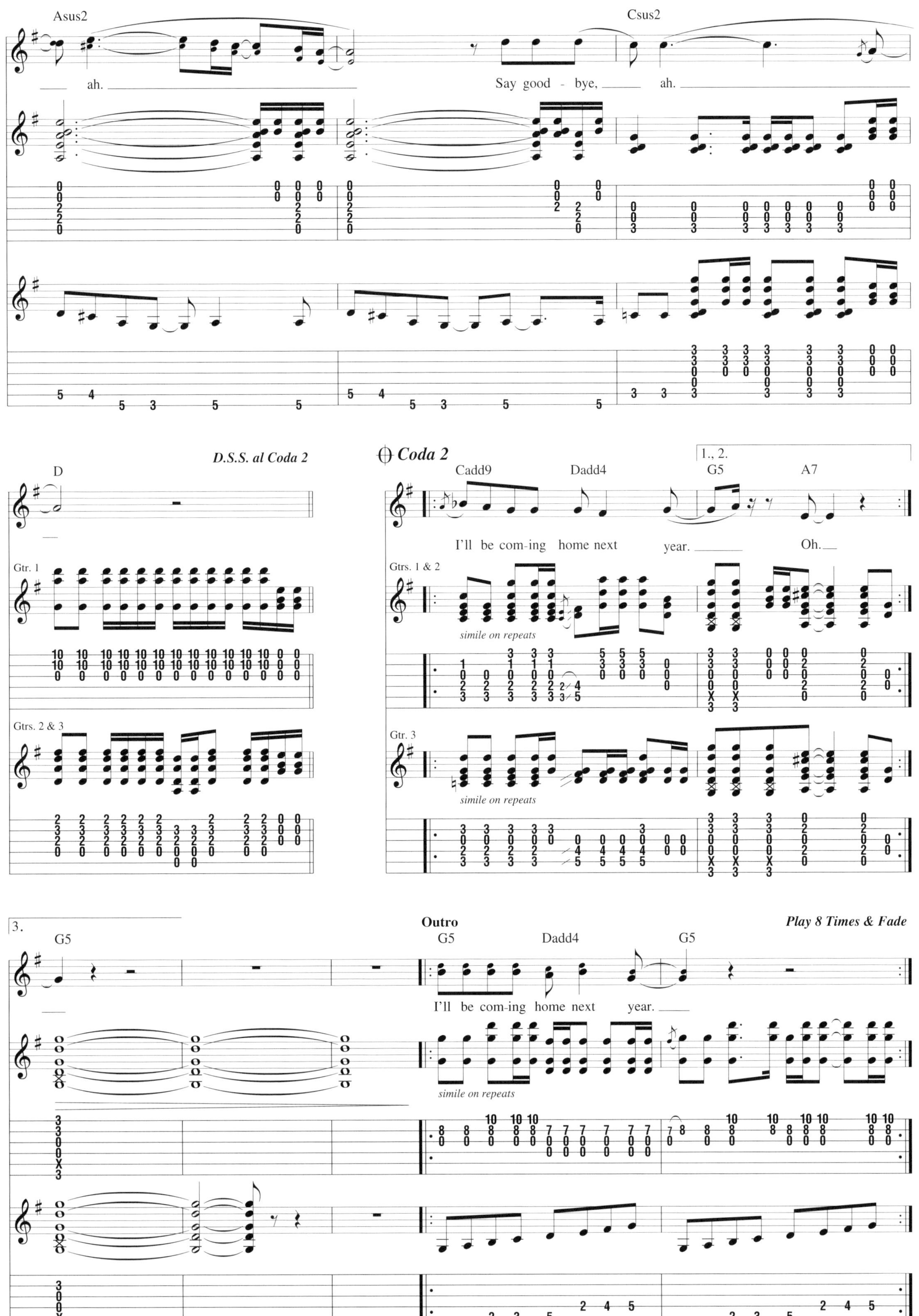
Asus2
Csus2
ah.
Say good - bye,
ah.
D
D.S.S. al Coda 2
Coda 2
Cadd9
Dadd4
1., 2.
G5
A7
I'll be com-ing home next year.
Oh.
Gtr. 1
Gtrs. 2 & 3
Gtrs. 1 & 2
Gtr. 3
simile on repeats
3.
G5
Outro
G5
Dadd4
G5
Play 8 Times & Fade
I'll be com-ing home next year.

Headwires

Words and Music by Dave Grohl, Nate Mendel and Taylor Hawkins

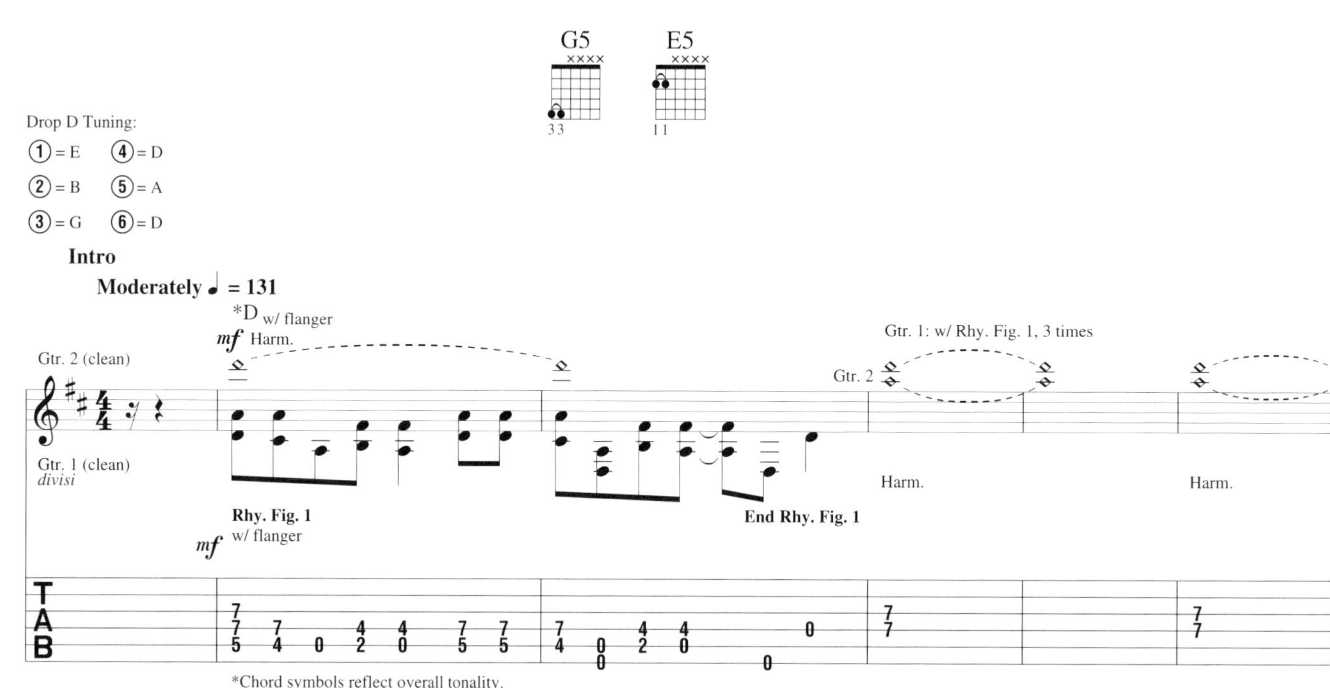

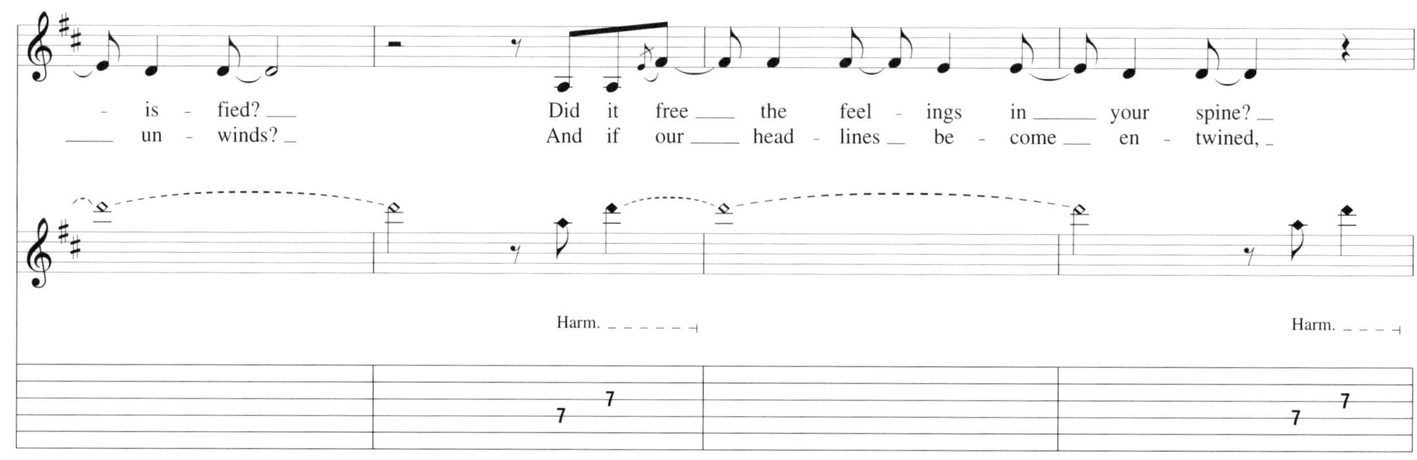

G
E5
D
Sleep - ing way in - side all this time.
you can have all mine, I will find.
Will they reach
And the rea -
Harm.
End Riff A
Gtr. 2
Gtr. 1
divisi
Rhy. Fig. 2
End Rhy. Fig. 2
Gtr. 1: w/ Rhy. Fig. 1, 3 times
Gtr. 2: w/ Riff A
your mind where the night col - lides?
- son why, keep - in' me a - live.
Will you greet your - self when the sun ar - rives?
There's a cure in me that I wish were mine.
Gtr. 1: w/ Rhy. Fig. 2
G
E5
D
Ob - jects stay be - hind. I've learned why.
Prob - lem is, I can't find my - self.
Chorus
B5
A5
G5
Bet-ter than a bul - let be - in' fired, tan - gled in your
Riff B
Gtr. 1
flanger off
simile on repeat
Rhy. Fig. 3
Gtr. 3 (dist.)
Gtrs. 3 & 4 (dist.)
f
Harm.
simile on repeat

C5
G/B
D
head
wires
now.
End Riff B
End Rhy. Fig. 3
Gtrs. 1, 3 & 4: w/ Riff B & Rhy. Fig. 3, simile
B5
A5
G5
Bet - ter than a bul - let be - in' fired,
To Coda
C5
G/B
tan - gled in your head wires,
B♭5
F/A
G5
E5
head wires now.
Gtr. 1
w/ flanger
Riff C
Harm.
Gtr. 2
End Riff C
Gtrs. 3 & 4
Gtrs. 3 & 4
divisi

Interlude

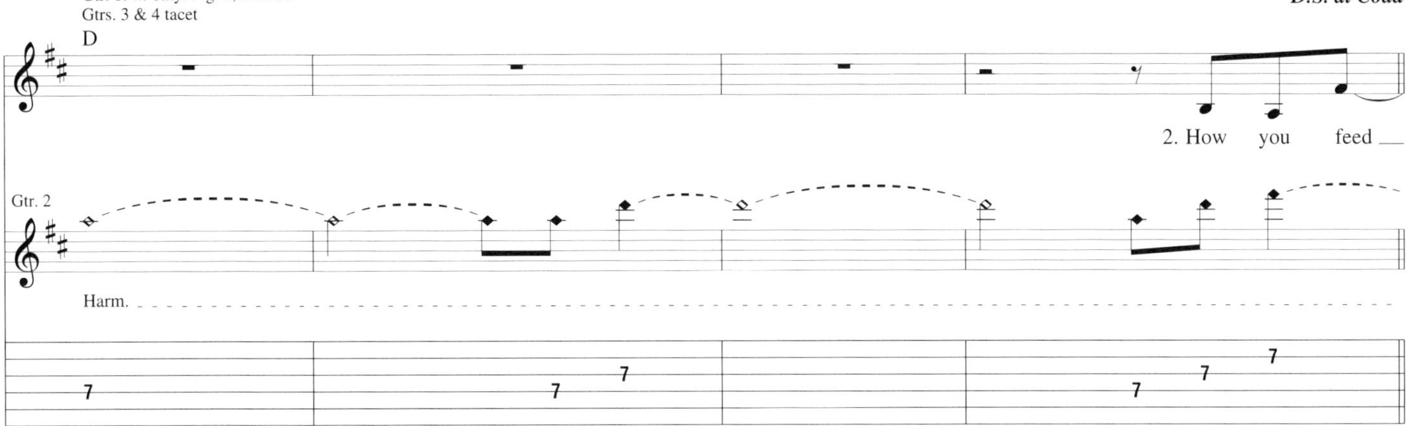
Gtr. 1: w/ Rhy. Fig. 1, 2 times
Gtrs. 3 & 4 tacet
D.S. al Coda
D
2. How you feed
Gtr. 2
Harm.

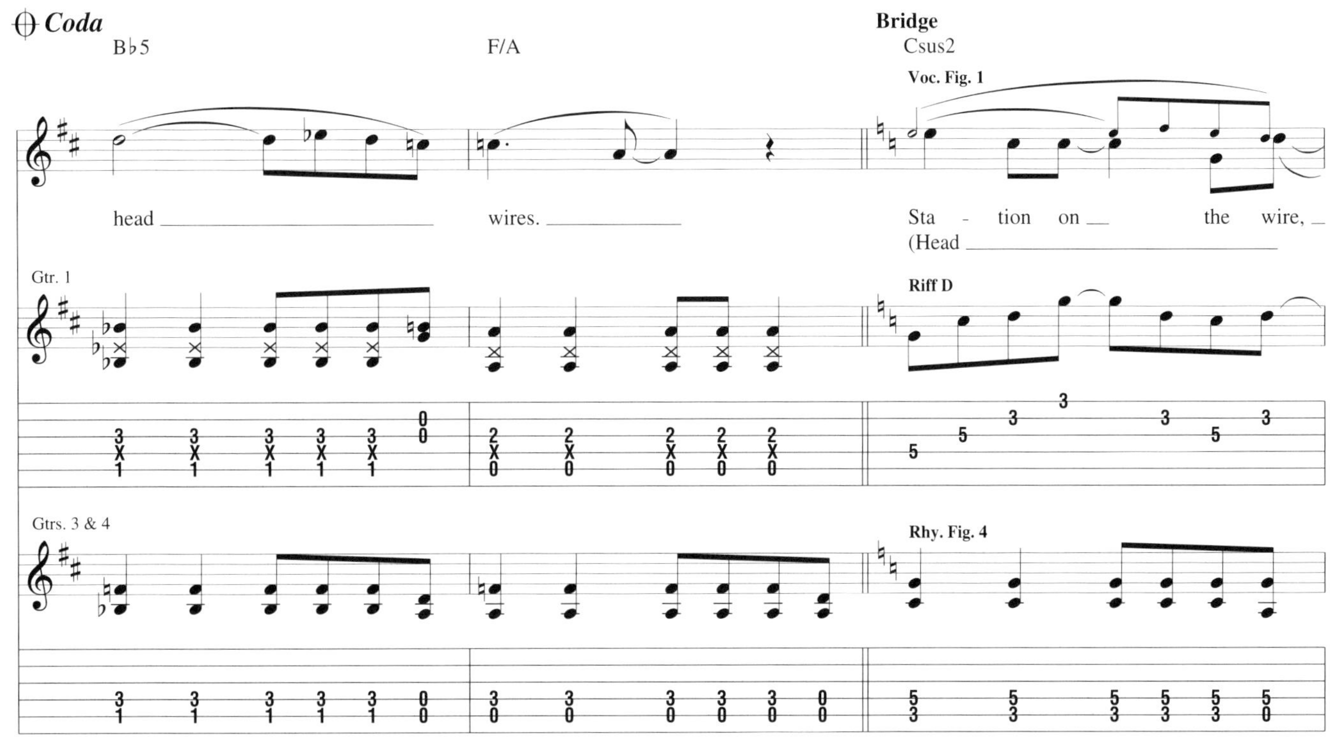
Coda
B♭5
F/A
Bridge
Csus2
Voc. Fig. 1
head
wires.
Sta - tion on the wire,
(Head
Gtr. 1
Riff D
Gtrs. 3 & 4
Rhy. Fig. 4

G/B
B♭sus2
F/A
End Voc. Fig. 1
one they all let go.
wires,
head
wires.)
End Riff D
End Rhy. Fig. 4

Bkgd. Voc.: w/ Voc. Fig. 1, 3 times
Gtr. 1: w/ Riff D, 2 3/4 times
Gtrs. 3 & 4: w/ Rhy. Fig. 4, 3 times, simile

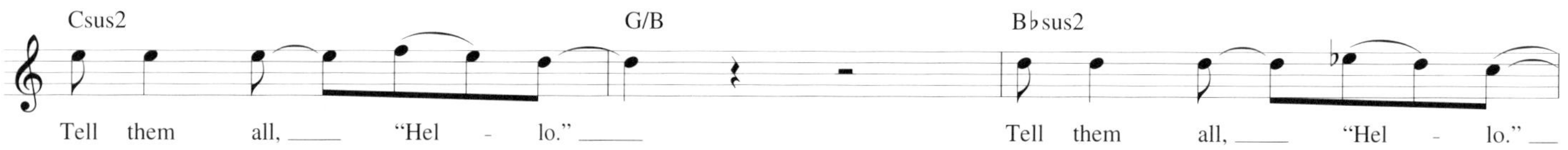

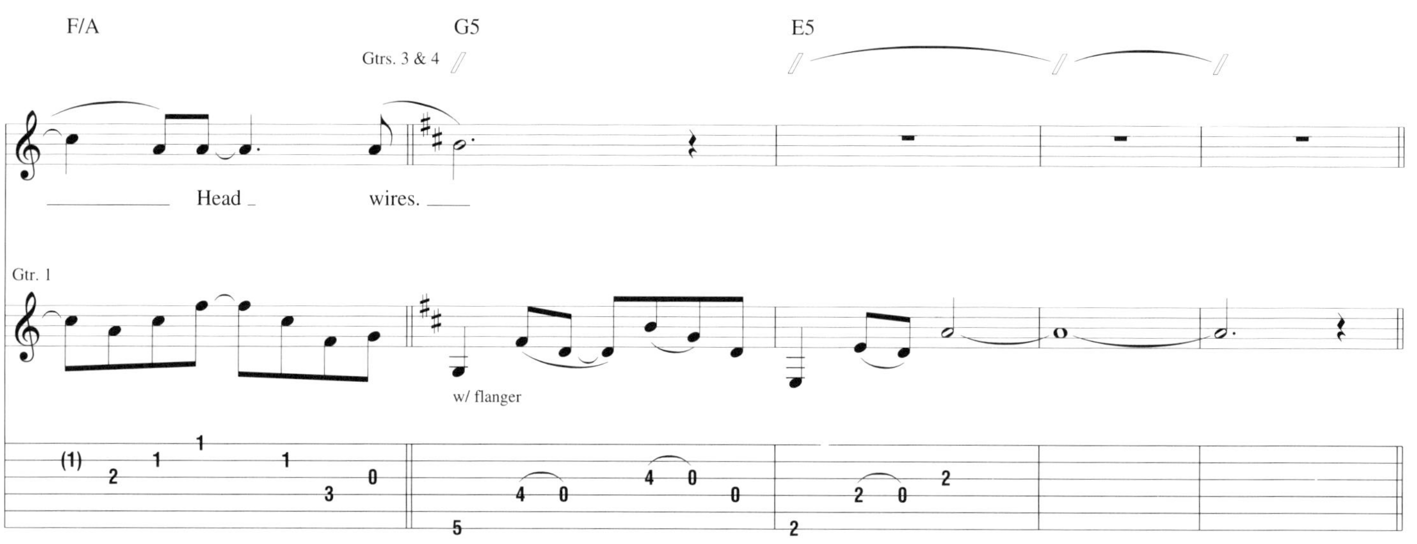

Interlude

Gtr. 1: w/ Rhy. Fig. 1, 4 times, simile
Gtrs. 3 & 4 tacet

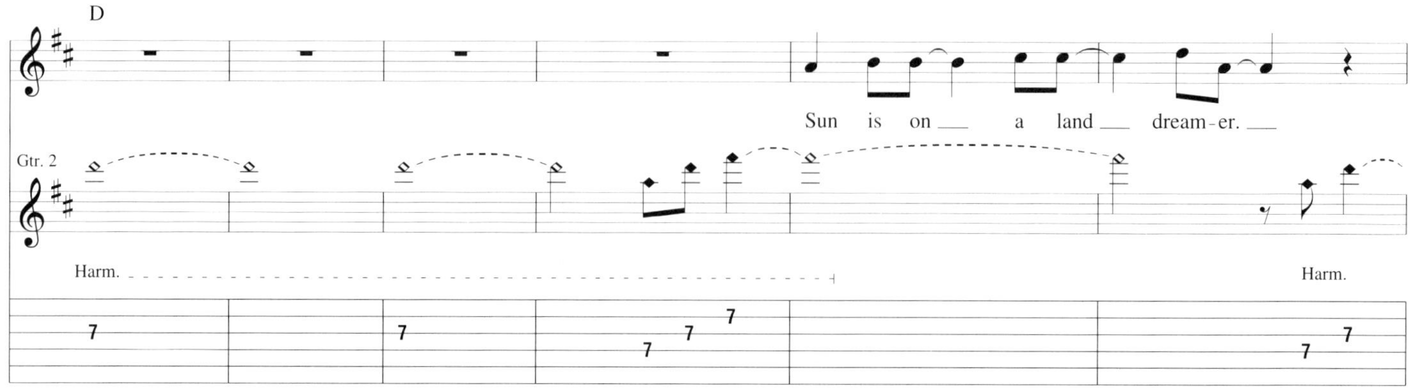

Gtr. 2: w/ Riff C
G
E5
Sun is on a land dream-er. Head wires, head wires.
Gtr. 1
Riff E
End Riff E
Harm.
Gtr. 1: w/ Rhy. Fig. 1, 2 times
D
Sun is on a land dream-er. Sun is on a land dream-er. Head - wires,
Gtr. 2
Riff F
Harm.
Harm.
Harm.
Gtr. 1: w/ Riff E
G
E5
Gtr. 1: w/ Rhy. Fig. 1, 2 times
Gtr. 2: w/ Riff F
D
head wires. Sun is on a land dream - er.
End Riff F
Harm.
Gtr. 1: w/ Riff E
G
E5
Sun is on a land dream-er. Head wires, head wires.
Gtrs. 3 & 4
mp
f
slight P.M.

Outro

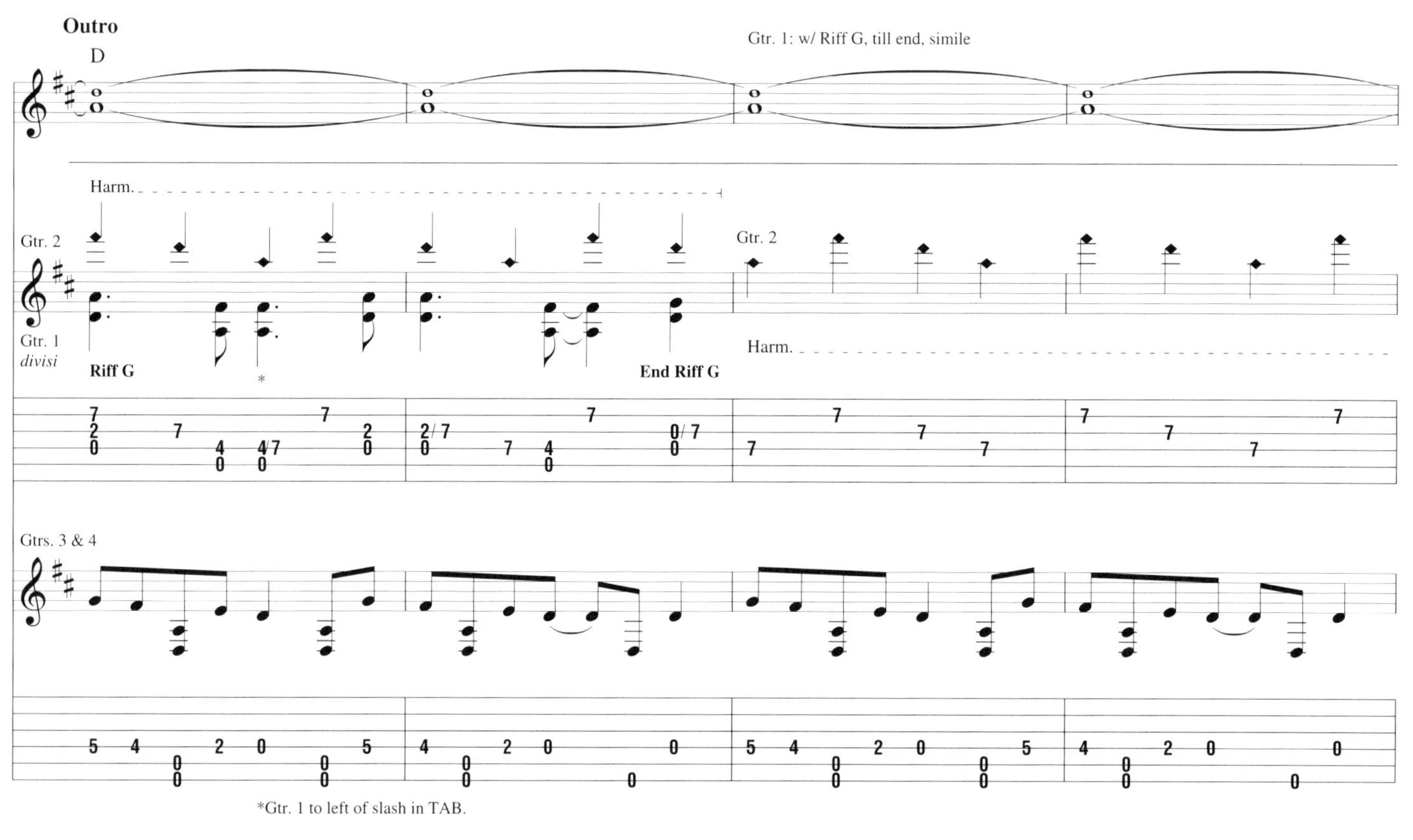

*Gtr. 1 to left of slash in TAB.

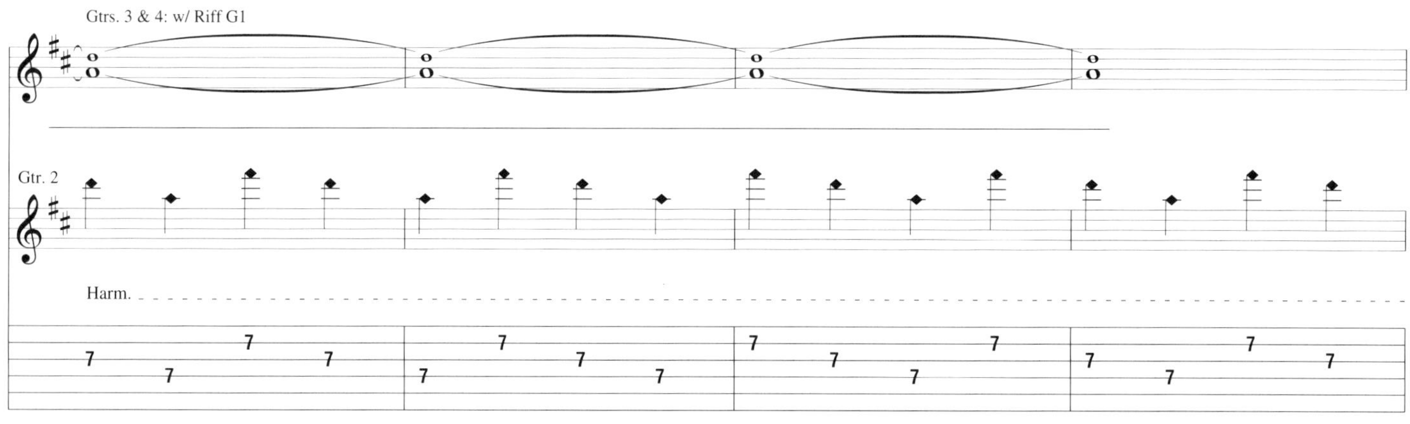

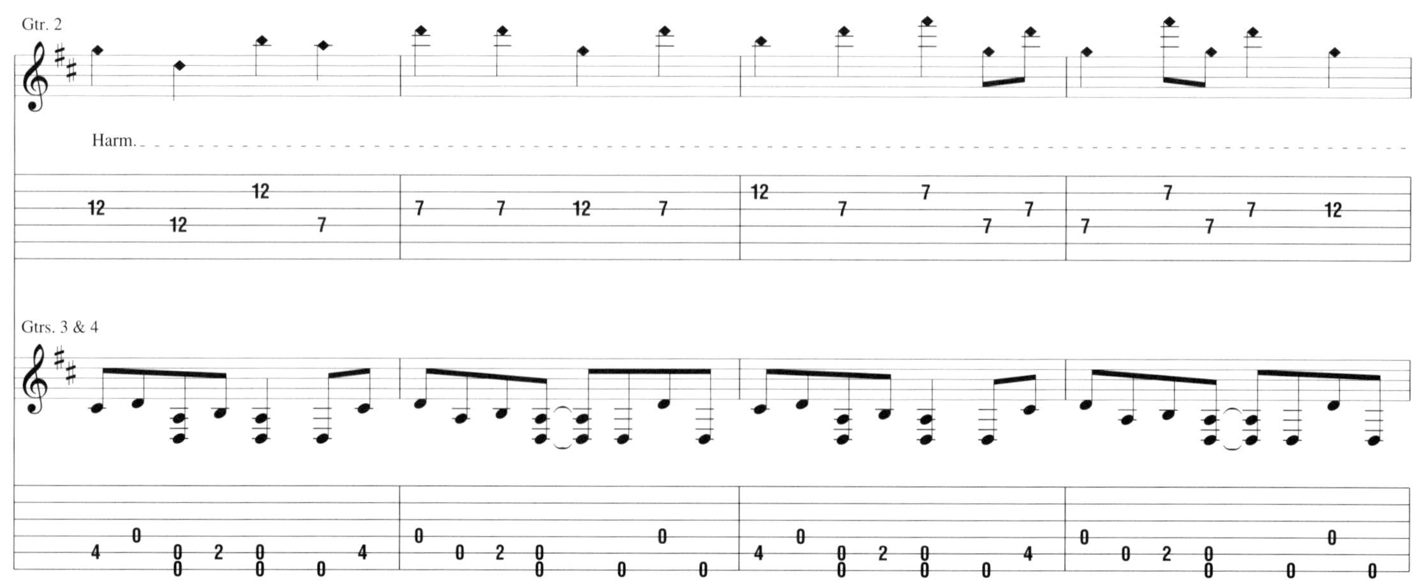

Begin Fade
Harm.
Harm.
Harm.
Fade Out

Ain't It the Life

Words and Music by Dave Grohl, Nate Mendel and Taylor Hawkins

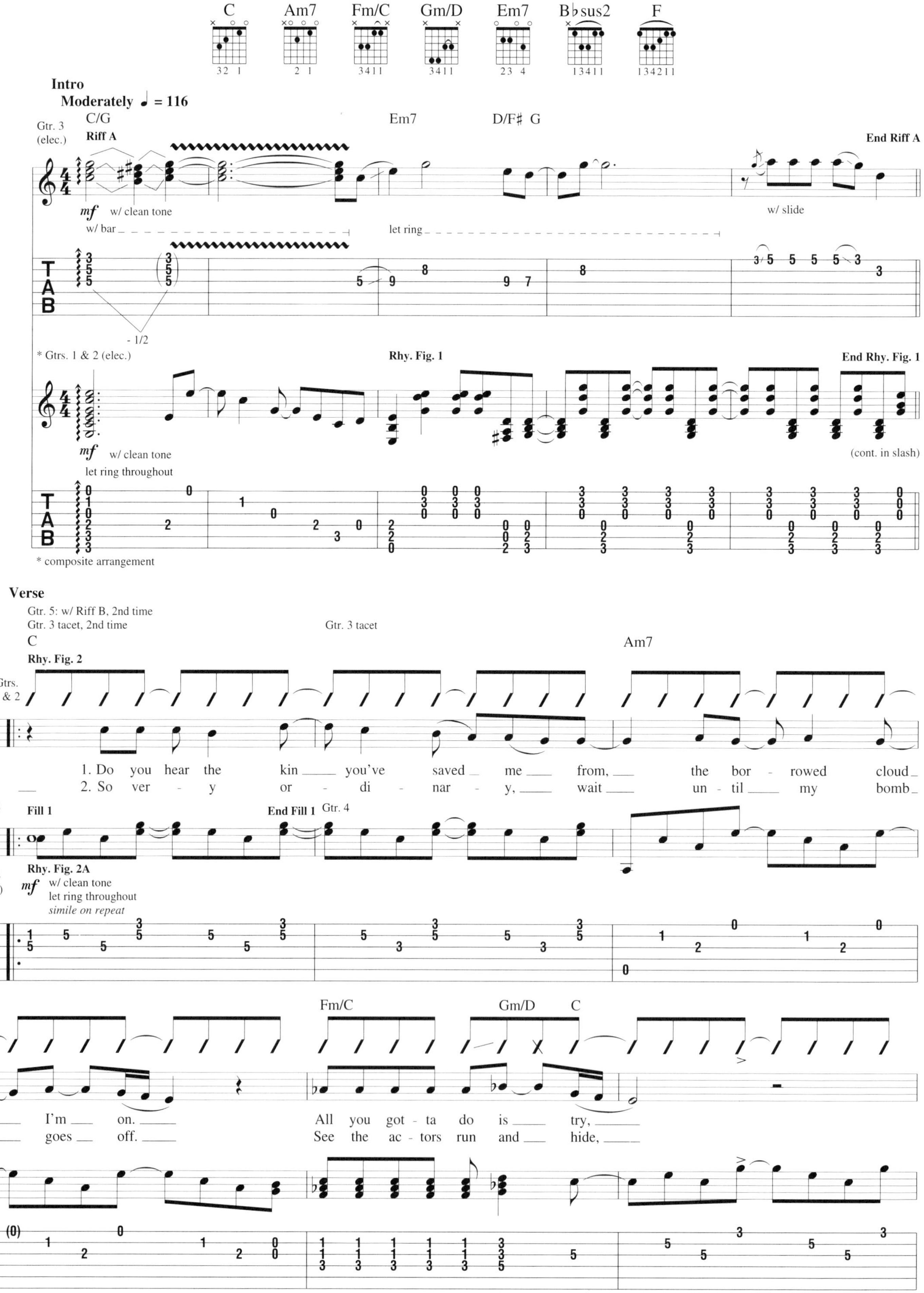

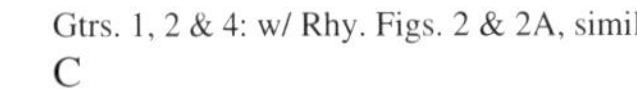
Gtrs. 1, 2 & 4: w/ Rhy. Figs. 2 & 2A, simile

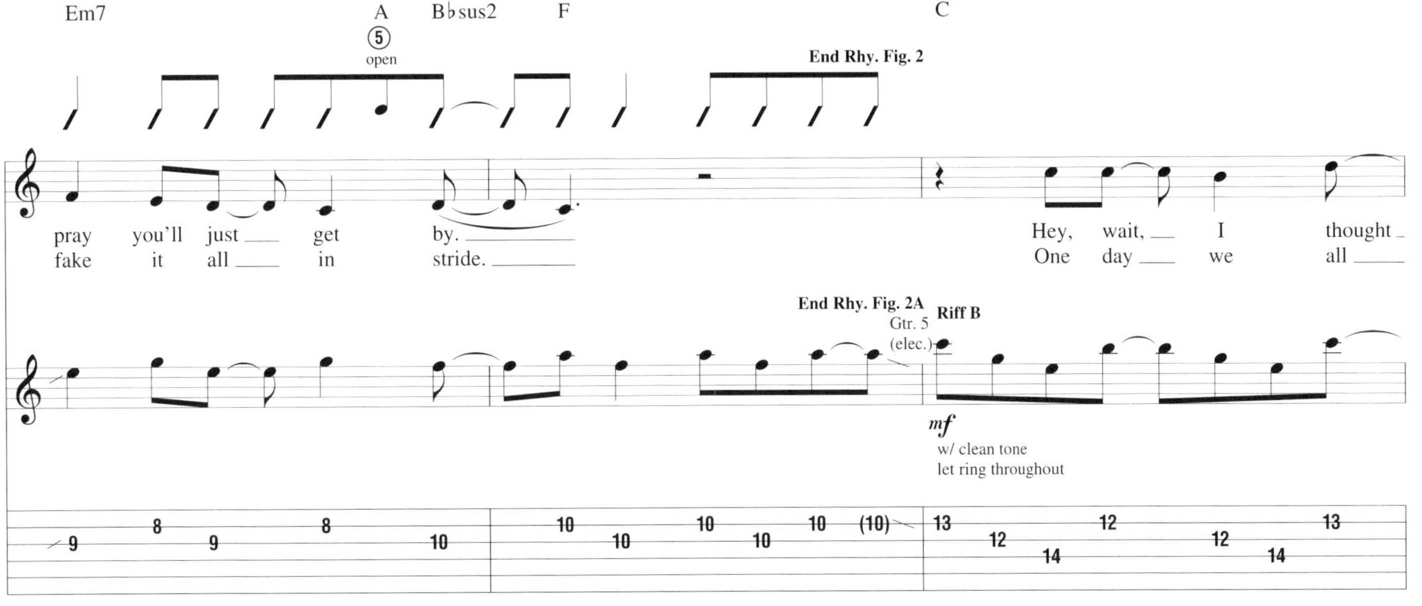
Em7
A
5
open
B♭sus2
F
C
End Rhy. Fig. 2
pray you'll just get by.
fake it all in stride.
Hey, wait, I thought
One day we all
End Rhy. Fig. 2A
Gtr. 5 (elec.)
Riff B
mf
w/ clean tone
let ring throughout

Am7
you made it out, your bought old crown fall off.
can say we're gone and hard the ground we're thrown.
End Riff B

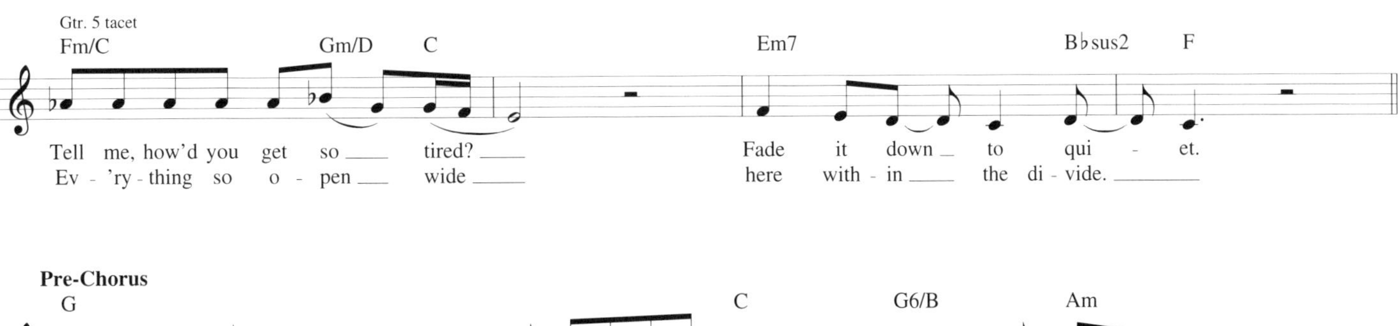
Gtr. 5 tacet
Fm/C
Gm/D
C
Em7
B♭sus2
F
Tell me, how'd you get so tired? Fade it down to qui - et.
Ev - 'ry - thing so o - pen wide here with - in the di - vide.

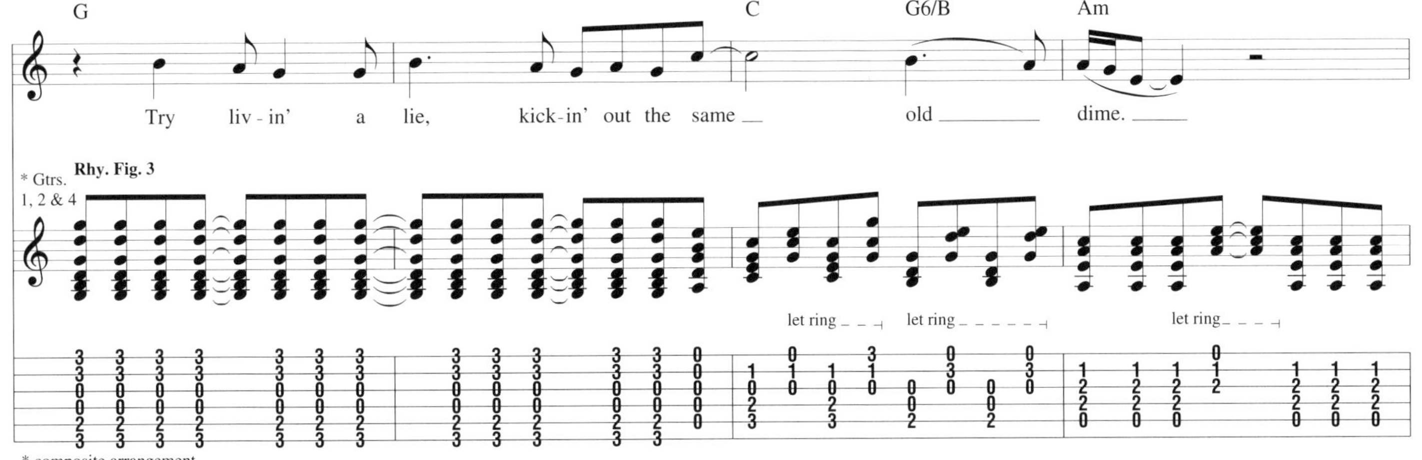
Pre-Chorus
G
C
G6/B
Am
Try liv - in' a lie, kick - in' out the same old dime.
* Gtrs. 1, 2 & 4
Rhy. Fig. 3
let ring
* composite arrangement

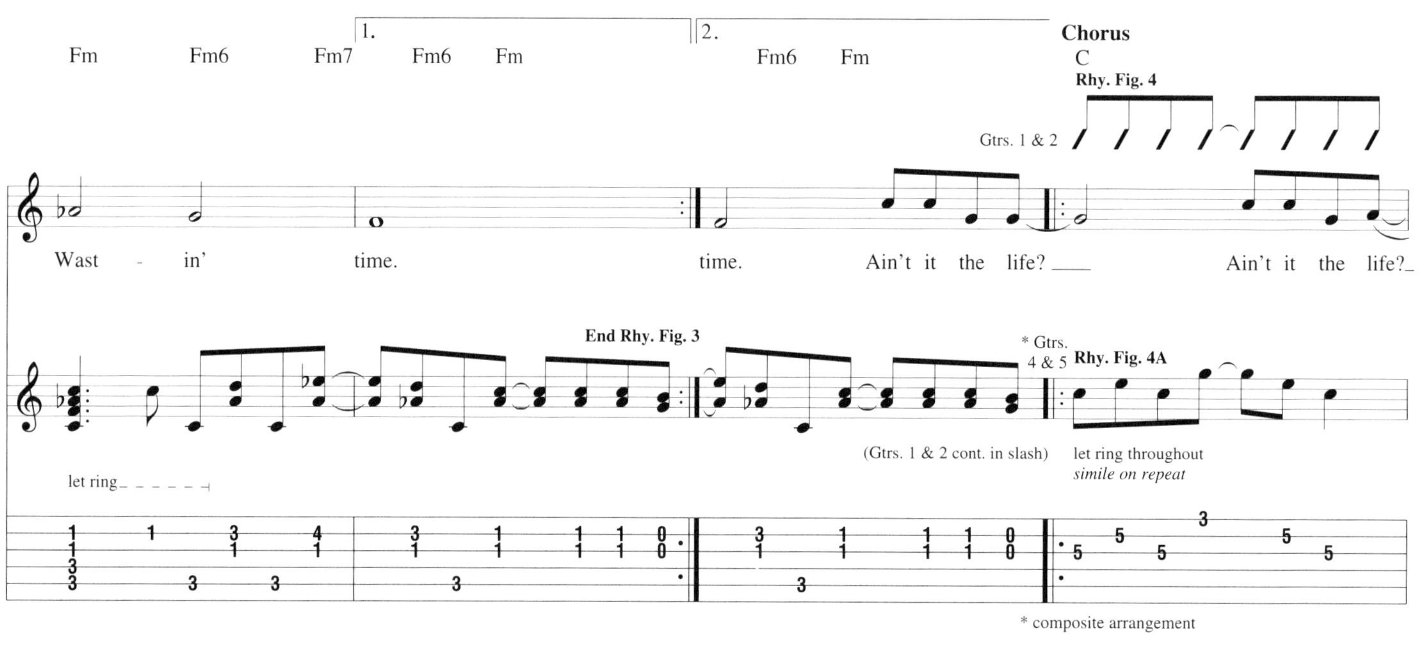
1.
2.
Chorus
Fm
Fm6
Fm7
Fm6
Fm
Fm6
Fm
C
Rhy. Fig. 4
Gtrs. 1 & 2
Wast - in' time. time. Ain't it the life? Ain't it the life?
End Rhy. Fig. 3
* Gtrs. 4 & 5
Rhy. Fig. 4A
let ring
(Gtrs. 1 & 2 cont. in slash)
let ring throughout
simile on repeat
* composite arrangement

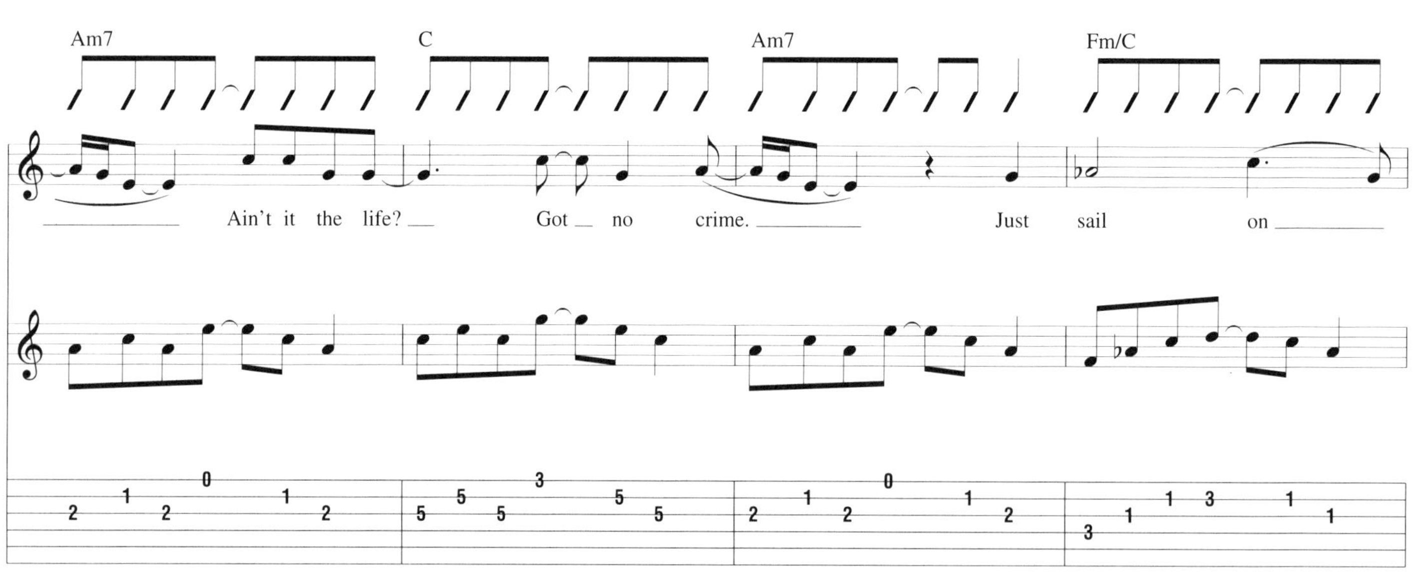
Am7
C
Am7
Fm/C
Ain't it the life? Got no crime. Just sail on

1.
2.
C
Em7
F
F
End Rhy. Fig. 4
by, sail on by. Ain't it the life? Ain't it the life?
End Rhy. Fig. 4A
Fill 2
End Fill 2
Gtrs. 4 & 5

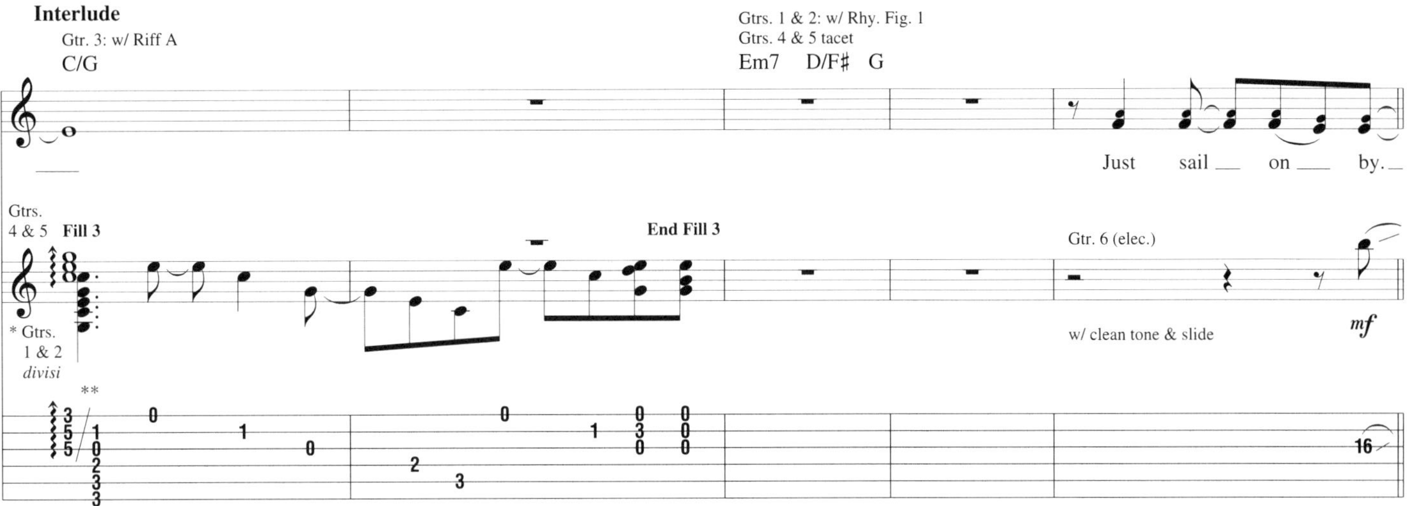

* composite arrangement
** Gtrs. 4 & 5 to left of slash in TAB.

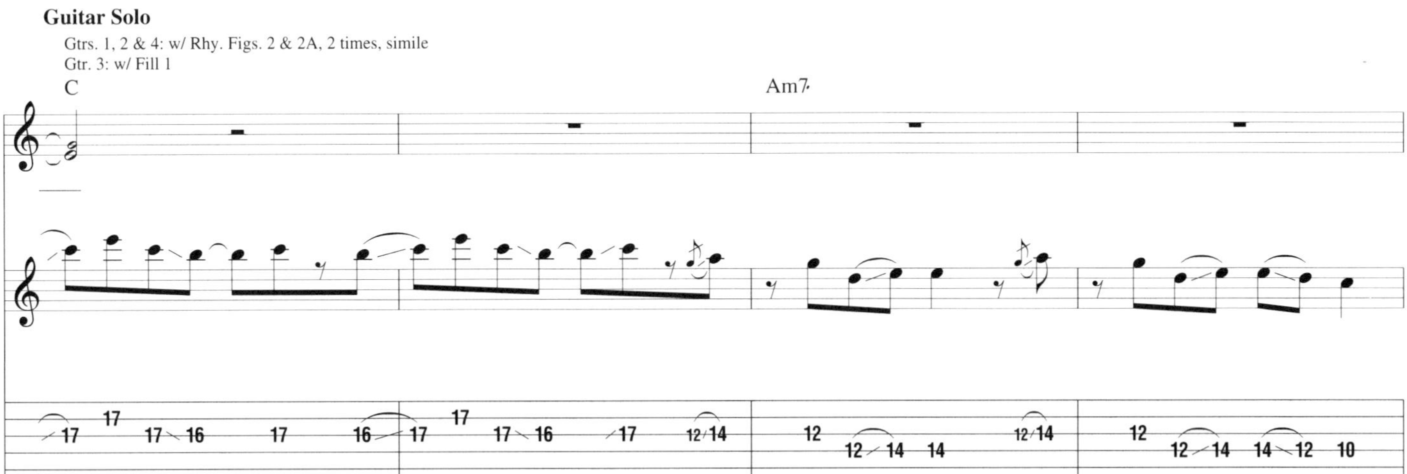

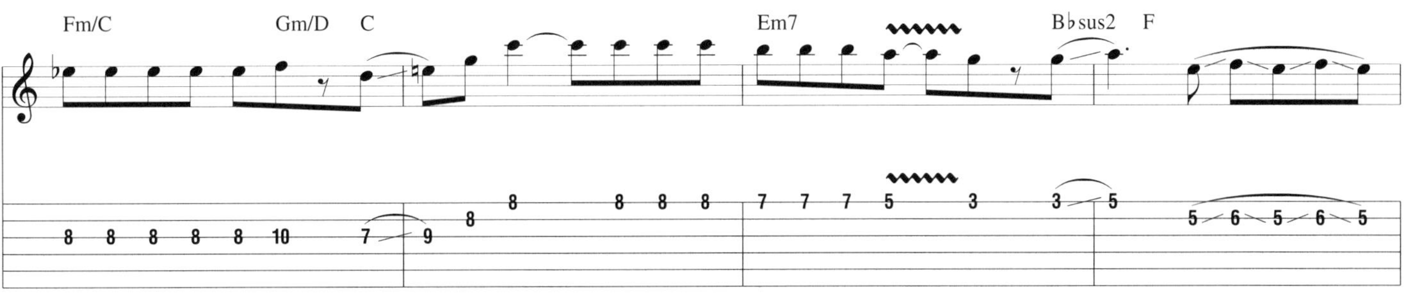

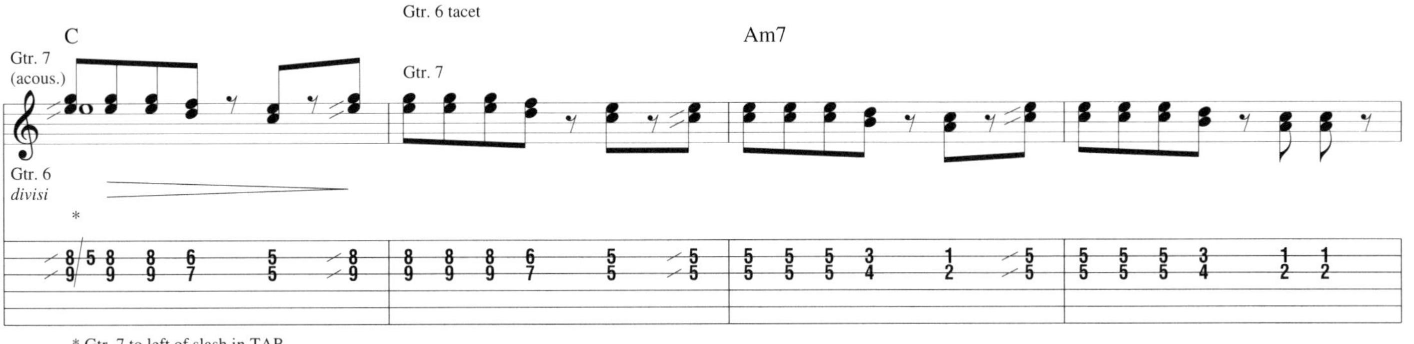

* Gtr. 7 to left of slash in TAB.

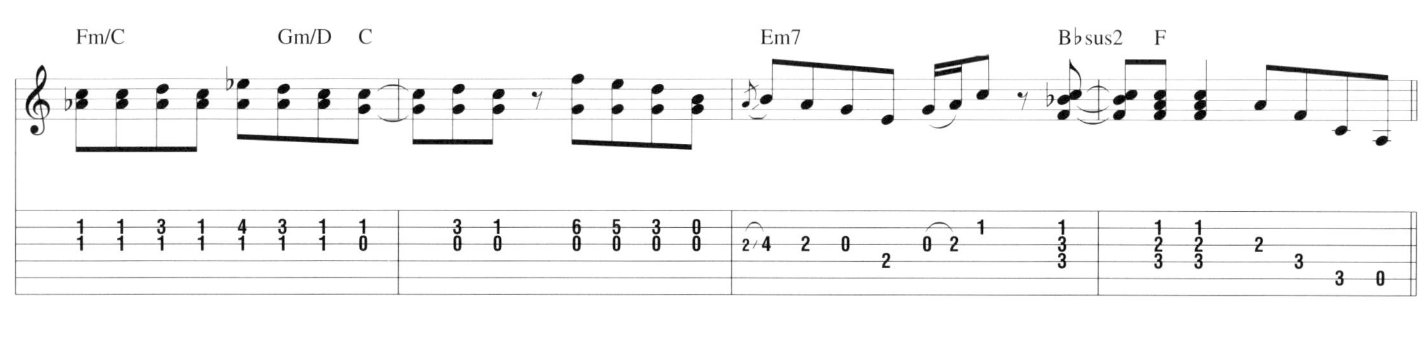
Fm/C
Gm/D C
Em7
B♭sus2 F

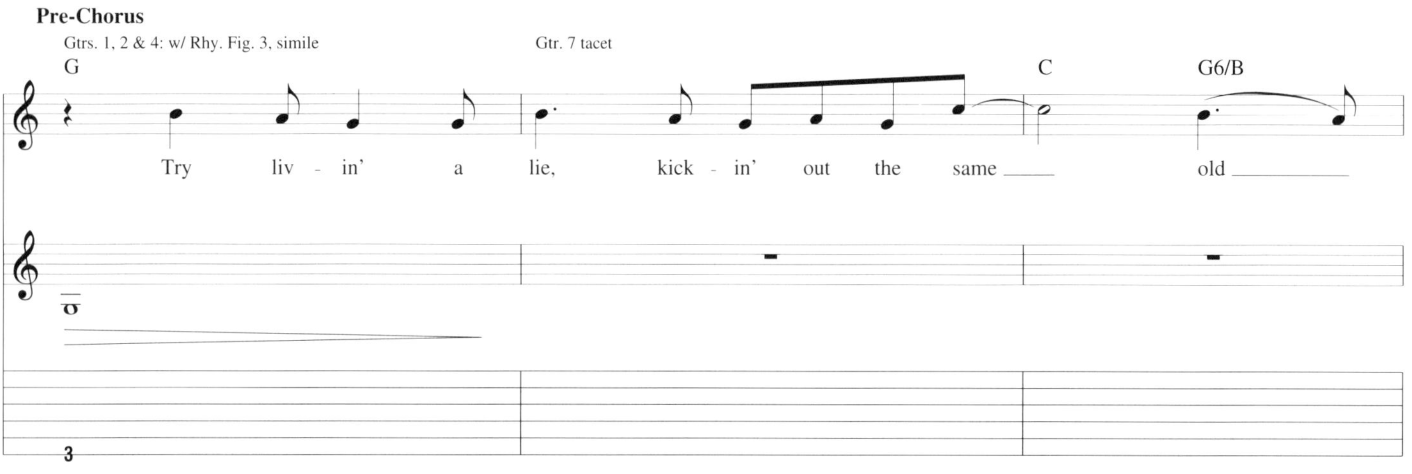
Pre-Chorus
Gtrs. 1, 2 & 4: w/ Rhy. Fig. 3, simile
Gtr. 7 tacet
G
C
G6/B
Try liv - in' a lie, kick - in' out the same old

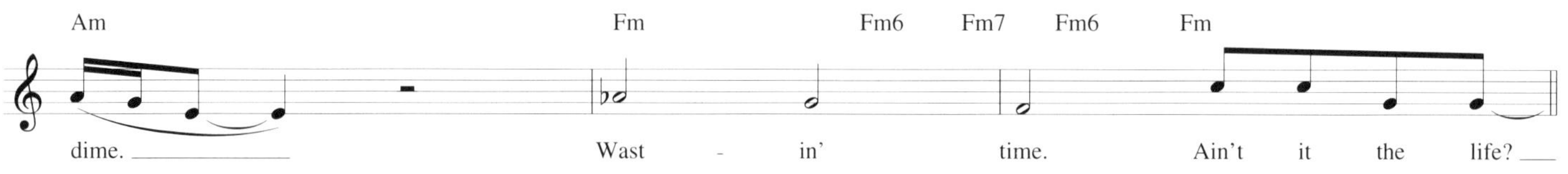
Am
Fm
Fm6 Fm7 Fm6
Fm
dime. Wast - in' time. Ain't it the life?

Chorus

Gtrs. 1 & 2: w/ Rhy. Fig. 4, 2 times
Gtrs. 4 & 5: w/ Rhy. Fig. 4A
C
Am7
C
Ain't it the life? Ain't it the life? Got no crime.
Gtr. 7
Riff C
End Riff C
mp

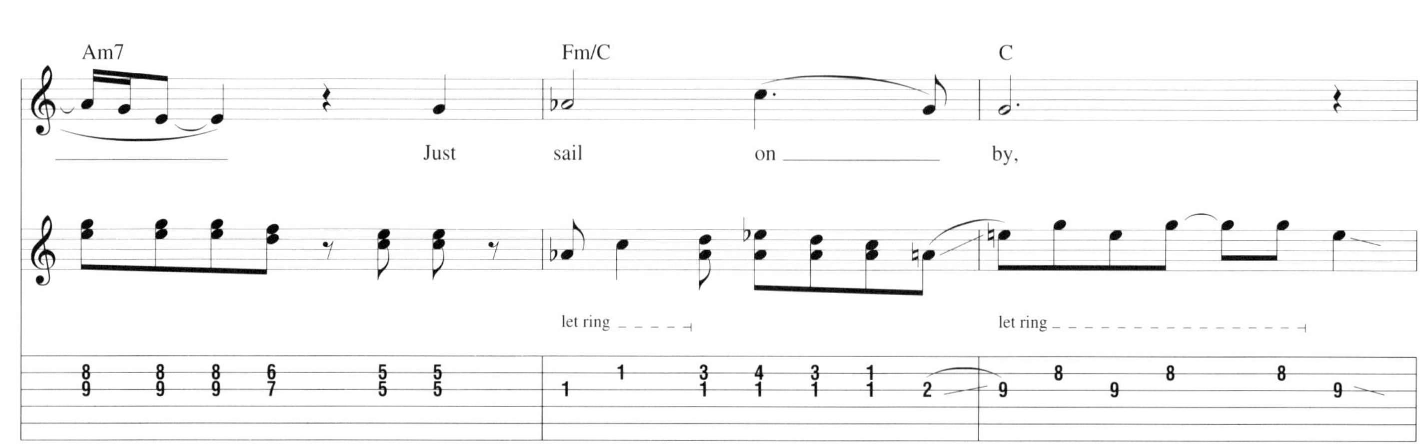
Am7
Fm/C
C
Just sail on by,
let ring
let ring

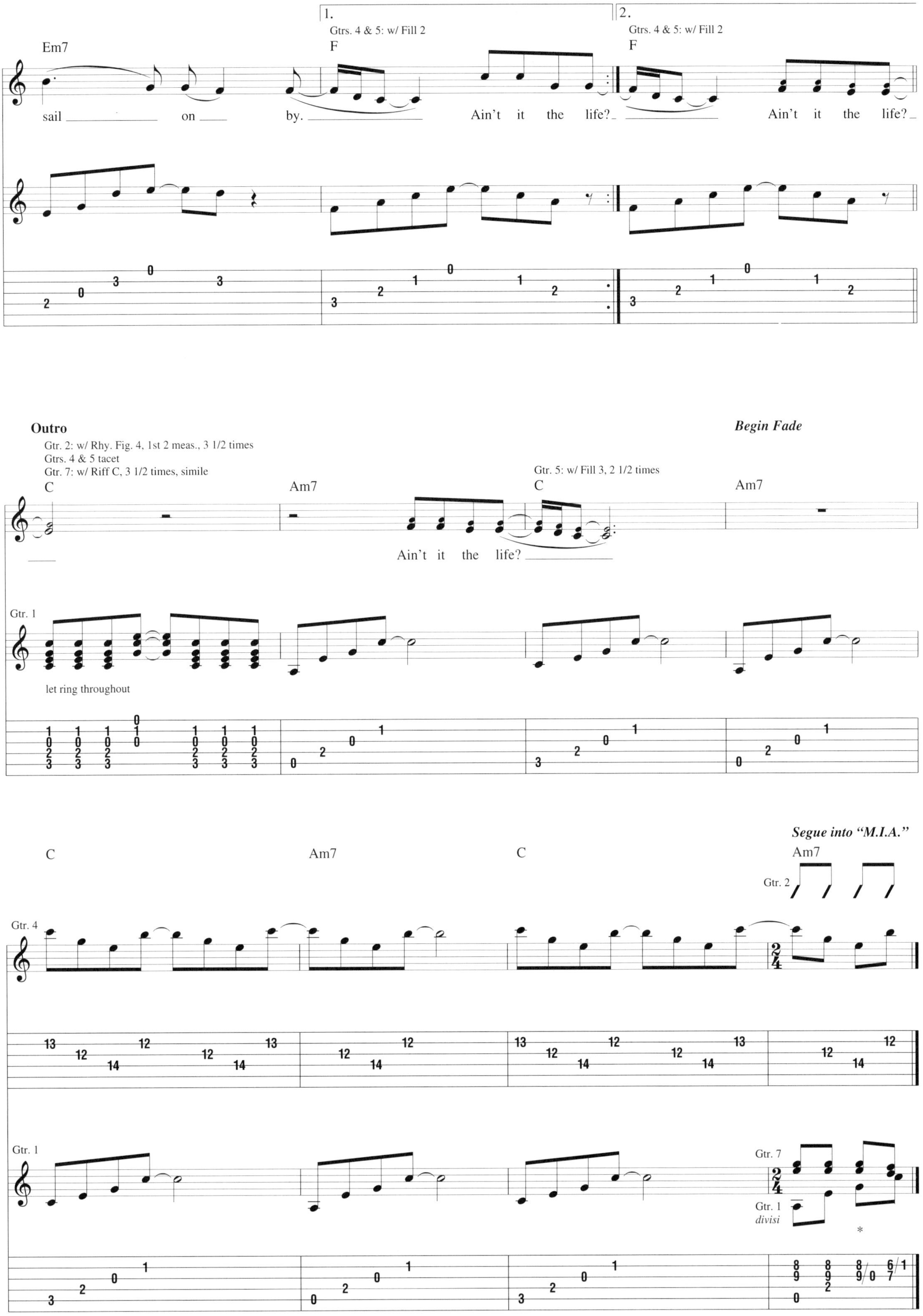

Outro

Begin Fade

Gtr. 2: w/ Rhy. Fig. 4, 1st 2 meas., 3 1/2 times
Gtrs. 4 & 5 tacet
Gtr. 7: w/ Riff C, 3 1/2 times, simile

Gtr. 5: w/ Fill 3, 2 1/2 times

C Am7 C Am7

Ain't it the life?

Gtr. 1

let ring throughout

Segue into "M.I.A."

C Am7 C Am7

Gtr. 2

Gtr. 4

Gtr. 1

Gtr. 7

Gtr. 1 *divisi*

* Gtr. 7 to left of slash in TAB.

M.I.A.

Words and Music by Dave Grohl, Nate Mendel and Taylor Hawkins

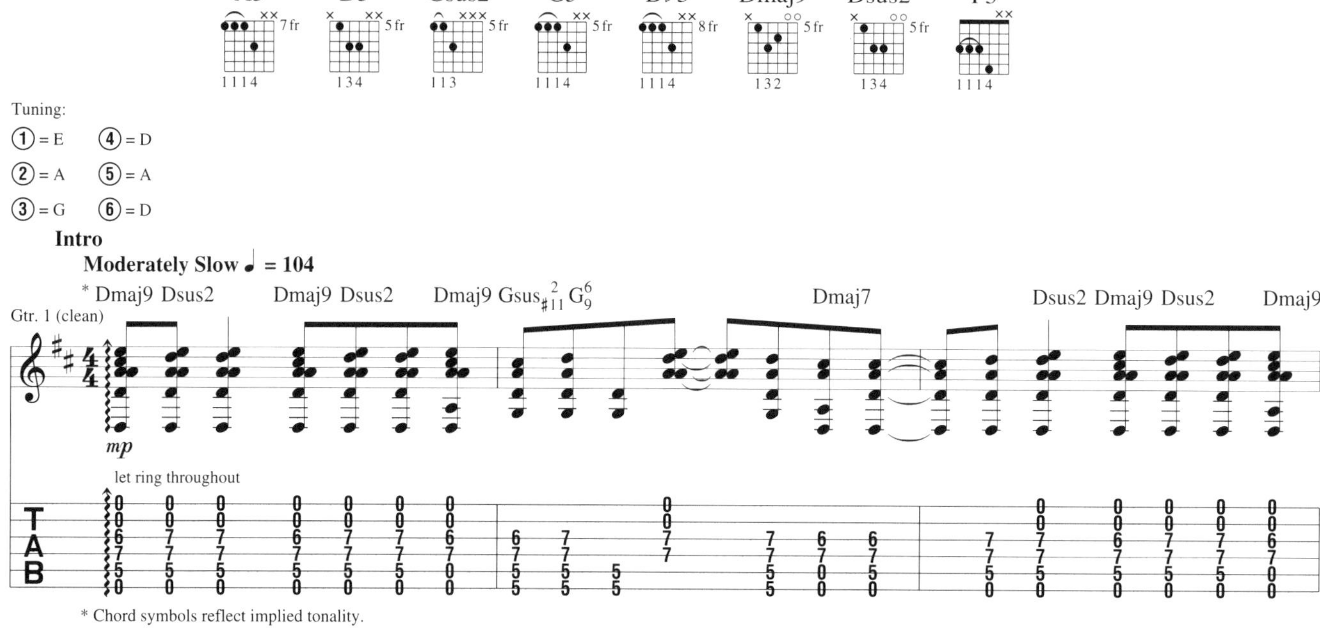

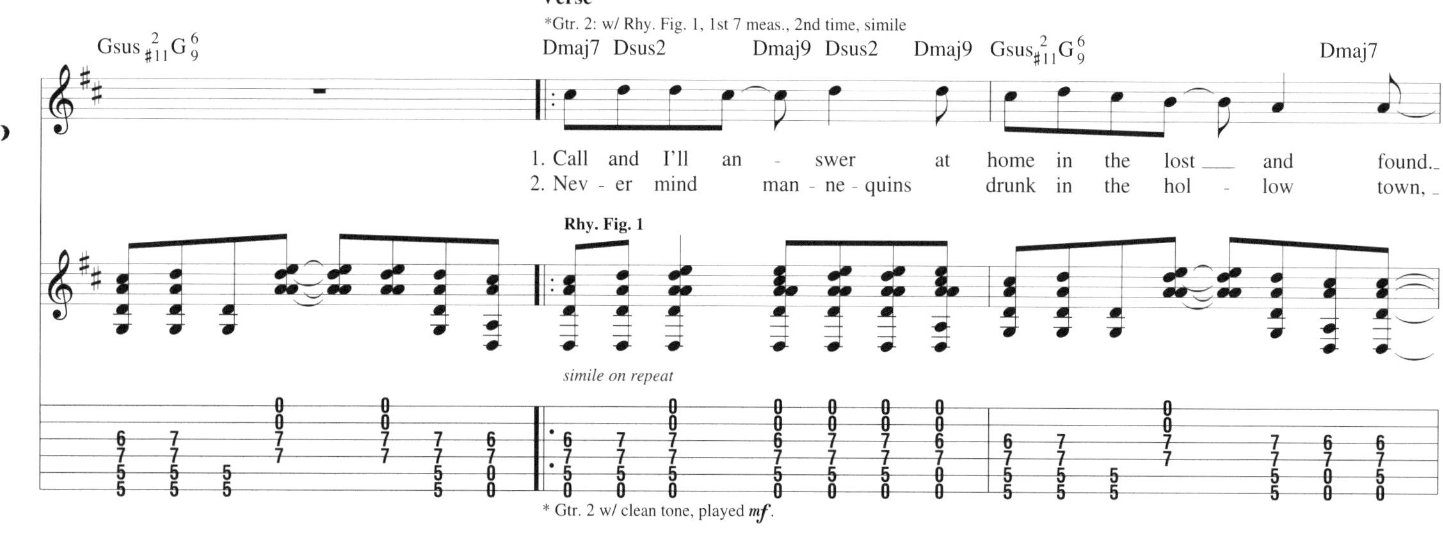

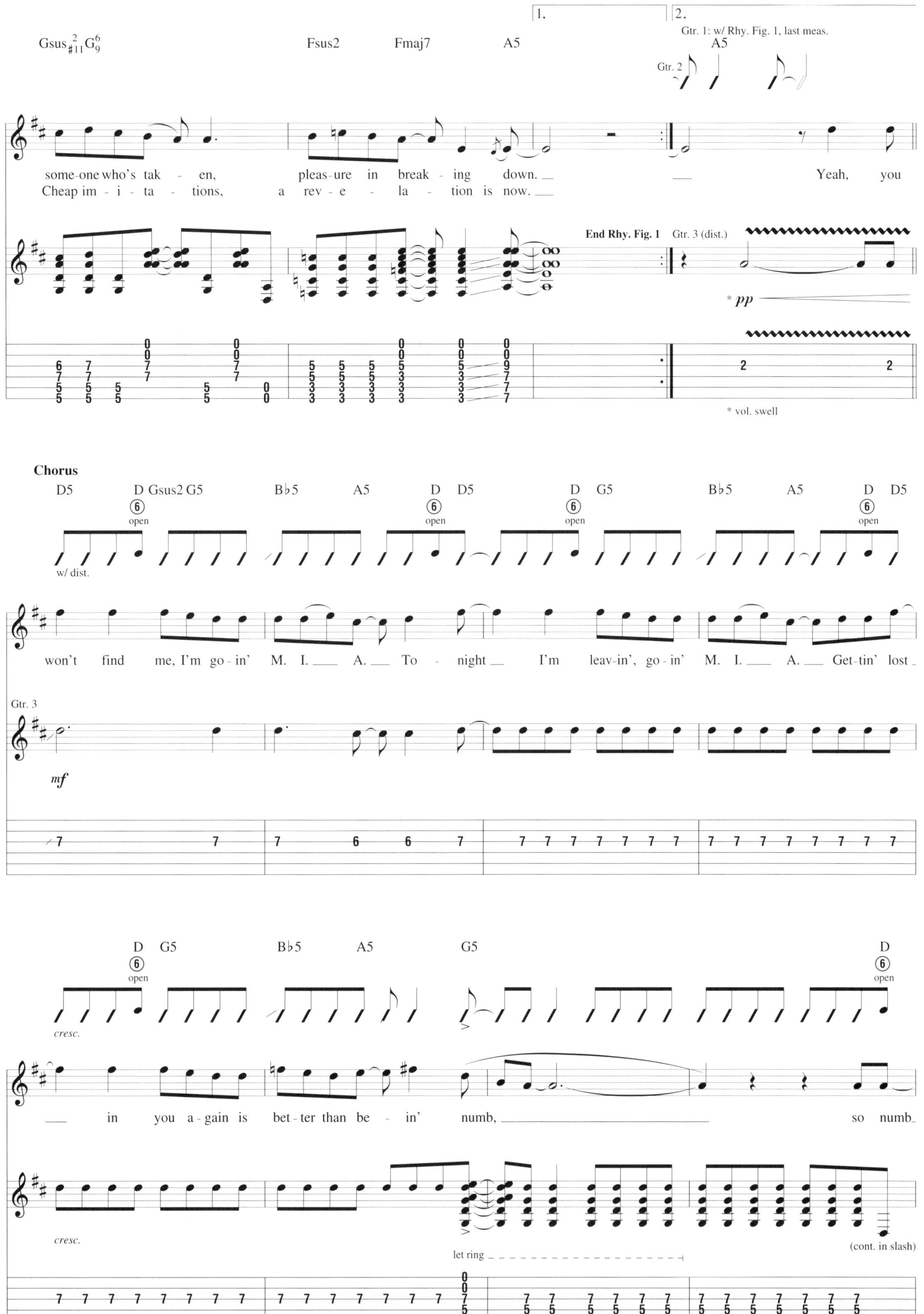
1.
2.
Gtr. 1: w/ Rhy. Fig. 1, last meas.
Gsus2#11 G6/9
Fsus2
Fmaj7
A5
A5
Gtr. 2
some-one who's tak - en, pleas-ure in break - ing down. __ __ Yeah, you
Cheap im - i - ta - tions, a rev - e - la - tion is now. __
End Rhy. Fig. 1
Gtr. 3 (dist.)
* pp
* vol. swell
Chorus
D5 D Gsus2 G5 B♭5 A5 D D5 D G5 B♭5 A5 D D5
open
w/ dist.
won't find me, I'm go - in' M. I. __ A. __ To - night __ I'm leav-in', go - in' M. I. __ A. __ Get-tin' lost
Gtr. 3
mf
D G5 B♭5 A5 G5 D
open
cresc.
__ in you a - gain is bet - ter than be - in' numb, __ so numb
cresc.
let ring
(cont. in slash)

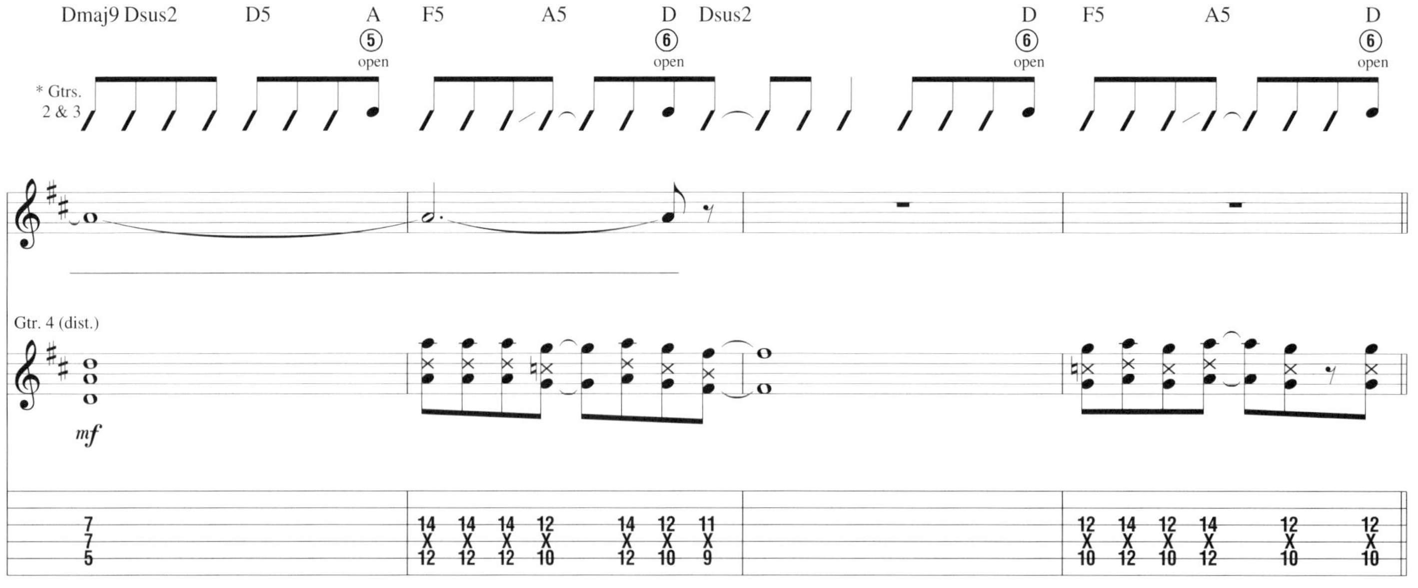

* composite arrangement

Verse

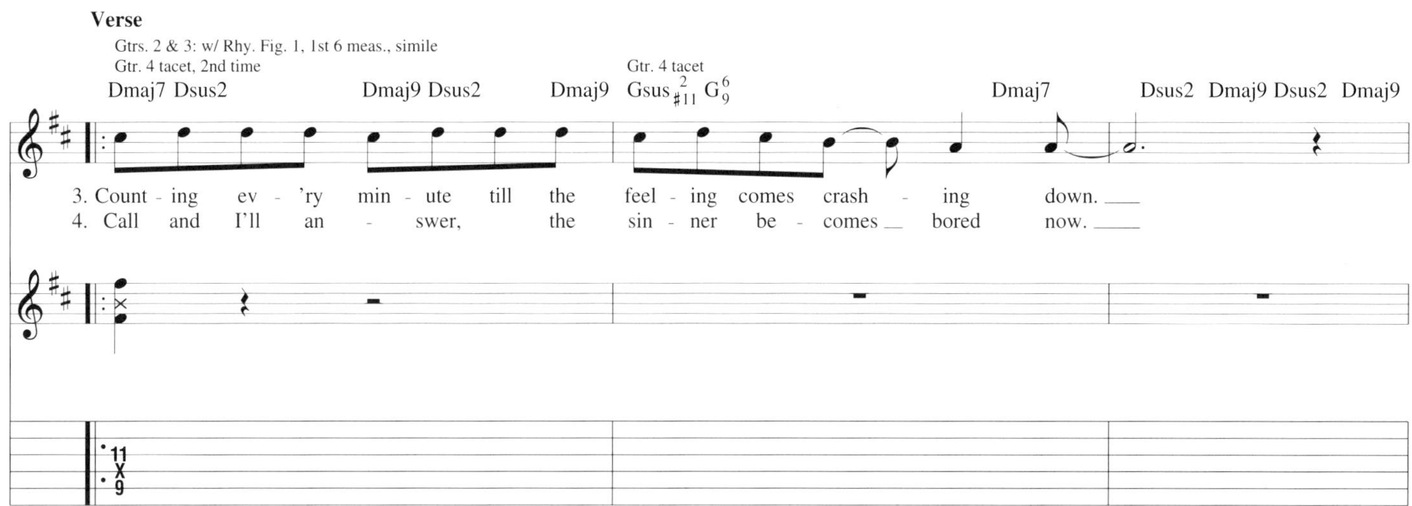

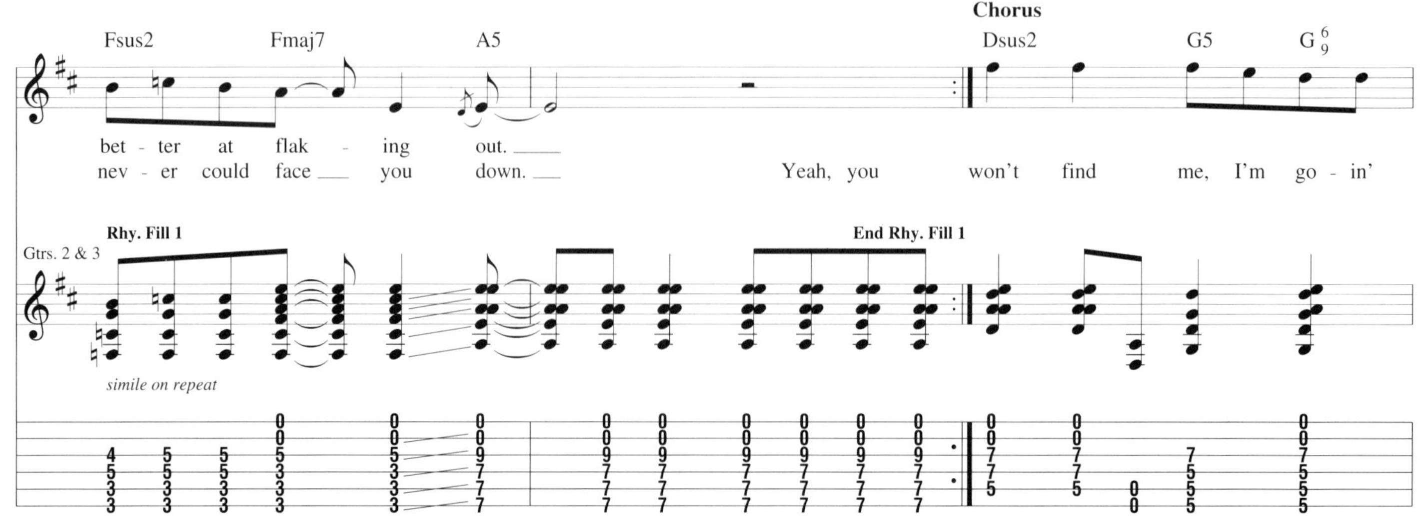

B♭5 A5 Dsus2 G5 B♭5 A5
M. I. A. To - night I'm leav - in', go - in' M. I. A. Get - tin' lost
Dsus2 G5 B♭5 A5 G6/9 G5
Gtrs. 2 & 3
(cont. in notation)
in you a - gain is bet - ter than be - in' numb.
Gtr. 4
(cont. in slash)
let ring
Bridge
Dmaj9 Bm11 A G6/9
And when raced a - round your head.
Gtr. 4
mf
Gtrs. 2 & 3
mf
let ring throughout

Gtr. 4 tacet
G/D C/D A/D D G/D C/D A/D D
Could-n't res - cue, could - n't res - cue. Could-n't res - cue, could - n't res - cue.
Gtrs. 2 & 3
G/D C/G A/D D G9 6
Could-n't res - cue, could - n't res - cue, now.
grad. cresc.
f
let ring
Verse
Gtrs. 2 & 3: w/ Rhy. Fig. 1, 1st 6 meas., simile
Dmaj7 Dsus2 Dmaj9 Dsus2 Dmaj9 Gsus2#11 G9 6 Dmaj7 Dsus2 Dmaj9 Dsus2 Dmaj9 Gsus2#11 G9 6 Dmaj7
5. Call and I'll an - swer at home in the lost and found. You say that I'm much too proud,
Gtrs. 2 & 3: w/ Rhy. Fill 1
Dsus2 Dmaj9 Dsus2 Dmaj9 Gsus2#11 G9 6 Fsus2 Fmaj7 A5
some-one who's tak - en pleas-ure in break - ing down. Yeah, you
Chorus
Dsus2 G5 B♭5 A5 Dsus2 G5
won't find me, I'm go - in' M. I. A. To - night I'm leav - in' go - in'
to me, I'm go - in' M. I. A. I can find re - lief, I'm go - in'
Gtrs. 2 & 3

1.
B♭5 A5 Dsus2 G5 B♭5 A5 Dsus2
M. I. A. So you don't find me, I'm go - in' M. I. A. To - night
M. I. A. Get - tin' lost in you a - gain is
G5 B♭5 A5
I'm leav - in', go - in' M. I. A. Say good - bye
2.
B♭5 A5
bet - ter than be - in' numb,
G6/9 B♭5 A5 G6/9 B♭5 A5
bet - ter than be - in' numb, bet - ter than play - in' dumb.
G6/9

Guitar Notation Legend

Guitar Music can be notated three different ways: on a *musical staff*, in *tablature*, and in *rhythm slashes*.

RHYTHM SLASHES are written above the staff. Strum chords in the rhythm indicated. Use the chord diagrams found at the top of the first page of the transcription for the appropriate chord voicings. Round noteheads indicate single notes.

THE MUSICAL STAFF shows pitches and rhythms and is divided by bar lines into measures. Pitches are named after the first seven letters of the alphabet.

TABLATURE graphically represents the guitar fingerboard. Each horizontal line represents a a string, and each number represents a fret.

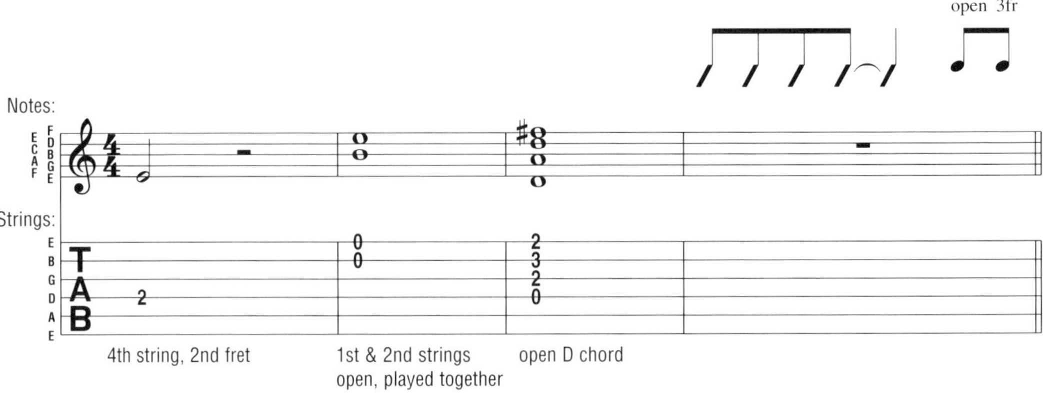

Definitions for Special Guitar Notation

HALF-STEP BEND: Strike the note and bend up 1/2 step.

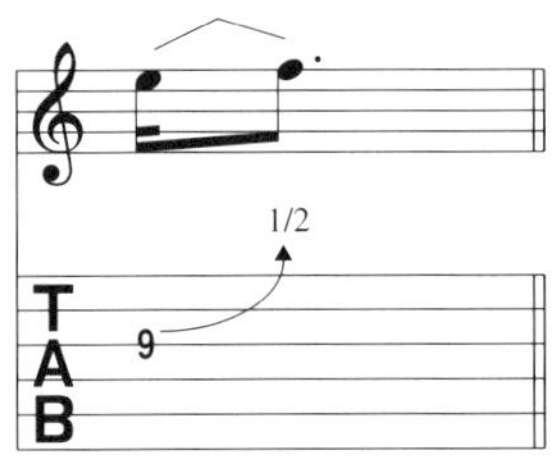

WHOLE-STEP BEND: Strike the note and bend up one step.

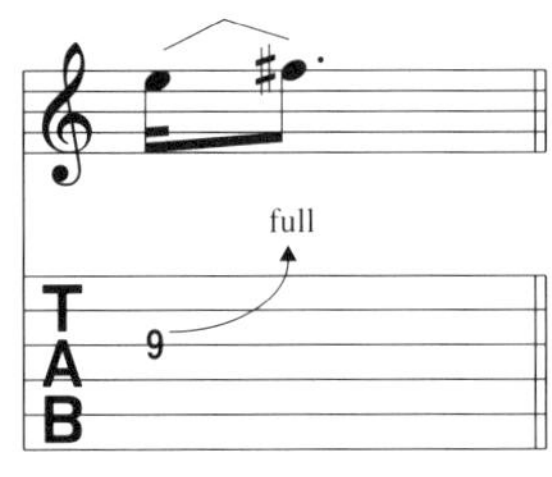

GRACE NOTE BEND: Strike the note and bend up as indicated. The first note does not take up any time.

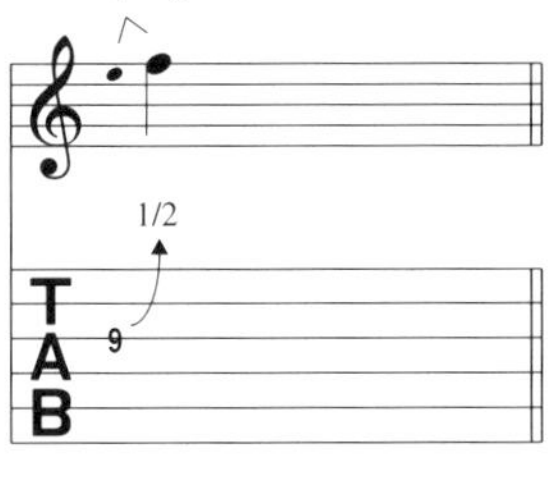

SLIGHT (MICROTONE) BEND: Strike the note and bend up 1/4 step.

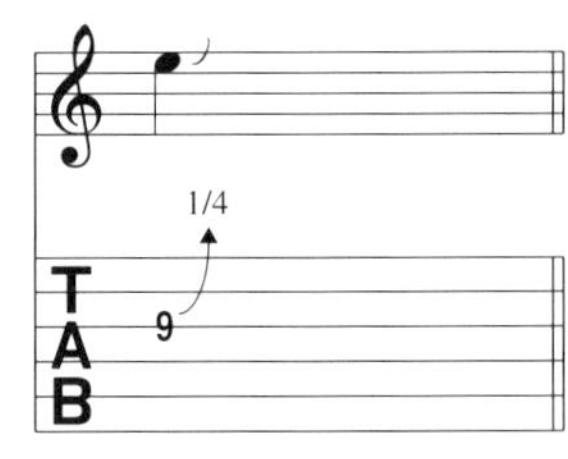

BEND AND RELEASE: Strike the note and bend up as indicated, then release back to the original note. Only the first note is struck.

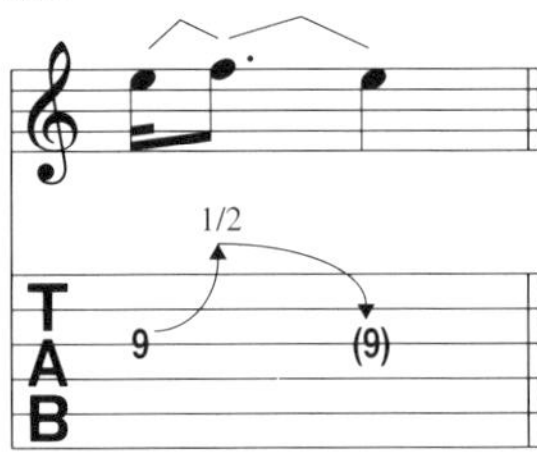

PRE-BEND: Bend the note as indicated, then strike it.

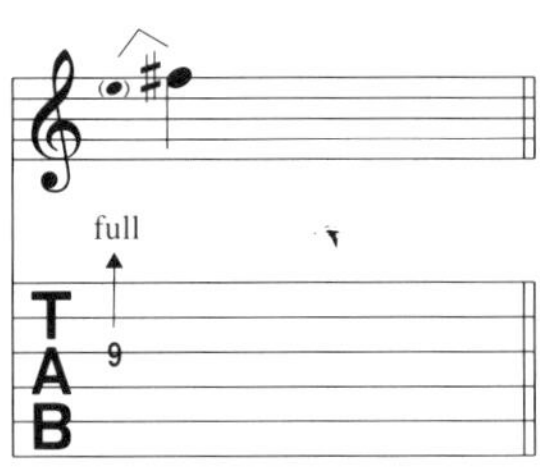

PRE-BEND AND RELEASE: Bend the note as indicated. Strike it and release the bend back to the original note.

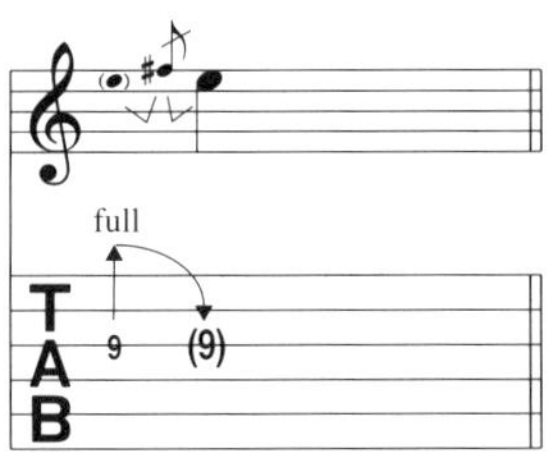

UNISON BEND: Strike the two notes simultaneously and bend the lower note up to the pitch of the higher.

VIBRATO: The string is vibrated by rapidly bending and releasing the note with the fretting hand.

WIDE VIBRATO: The pitch is varied to a greater degree by vibrating with the fretting hand.

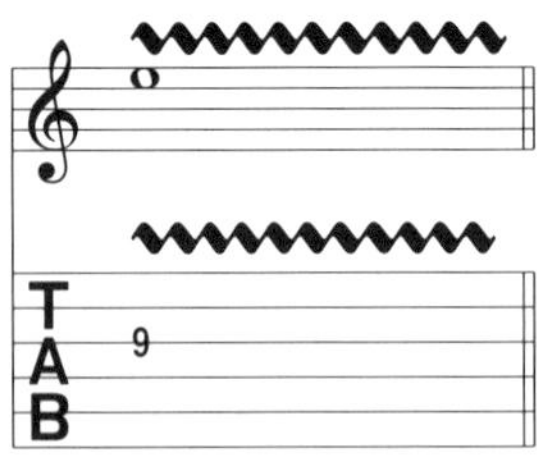

HAMMER-ON: Strike the first (lower) note with one finger, then sound the higher note (on the same string) with another finger by fretting it without picking.

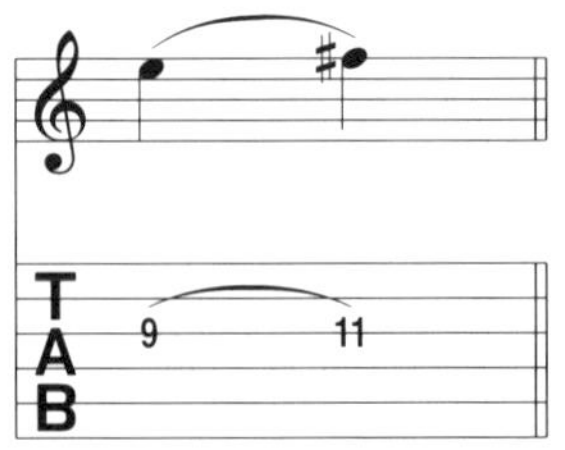

PULL-OFF: Place both fingers on the notes to be sounded. Strike the first note and without picking, pull the finger off to sound the second (lower) note.

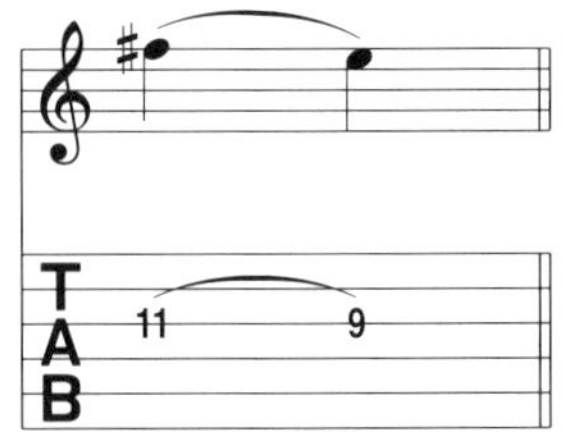

LEGATO SLIDE: Strike the first note and then slide the same fret-hand finger up or down to the second note. The second note is not struck.

SHIFT SLIDE: Same as legato slide, except the second note is struck.

TRILL: Very rapidly alternate between the notes indicated by continuously hammering on and pulling off.

TAPPING: Hammer ("tap") the fret indicated with the pick-hand index or middle finger and pull off to the note fretted by the fret hand.

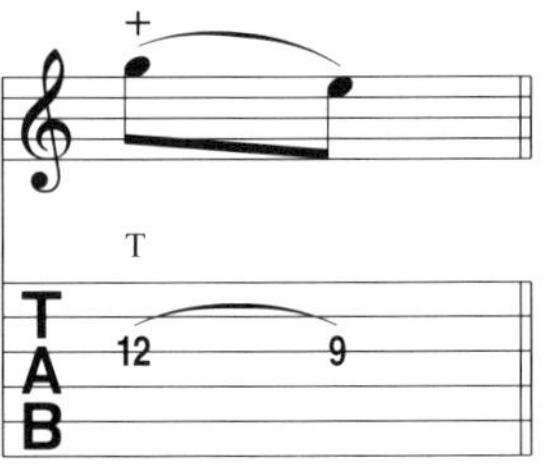

NATURAL HARMONIC: Strike the note while the fret-hand lightly touches the string directly over the fret indicated.

Harm.

12

PINCH HARMONIC: The note is fretted normally and a harmonic is produced by adding the edge of the thumb or the tip of the index finger of the pick hand to the normal pick attack.

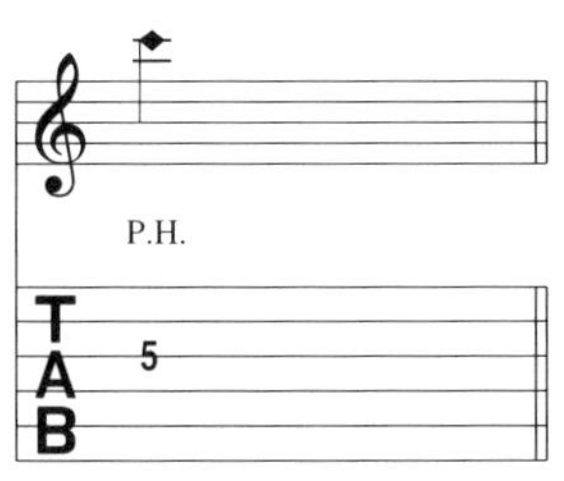

HARP HARMONIC: The note is fretted normally and a harmonic is produced by gently resting the pick hand's index finger directly above the indicated fret (in parentheses) while the pick hand's thumb or pick assists by plucking the appropriate string.

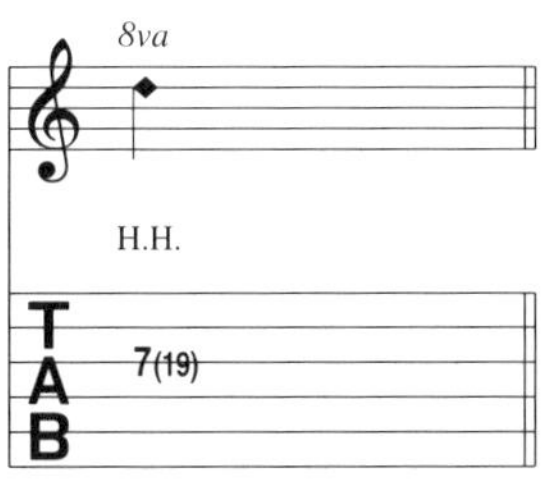

PICK SCRAPE: The edge of the pick is rubbed down (or up) the string, producing a scratchy sound.

MUFFLED STRINGS: A percussive sound is produced by laying the fret hand across the string(s) without depressing, and striking them with the pick hand.

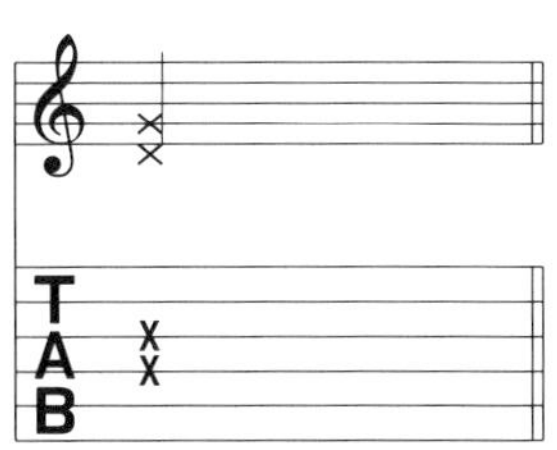

PALM MUTING: The note is partially muted by the pick hand lightly touching the string(s) just before the bridge.

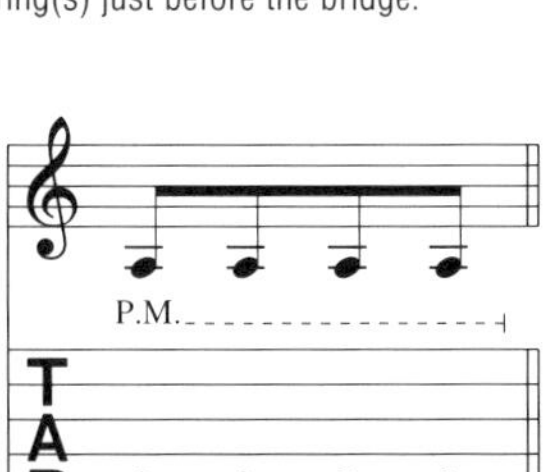

RAKE: Drag the pick across the strings indicated with a single motion.

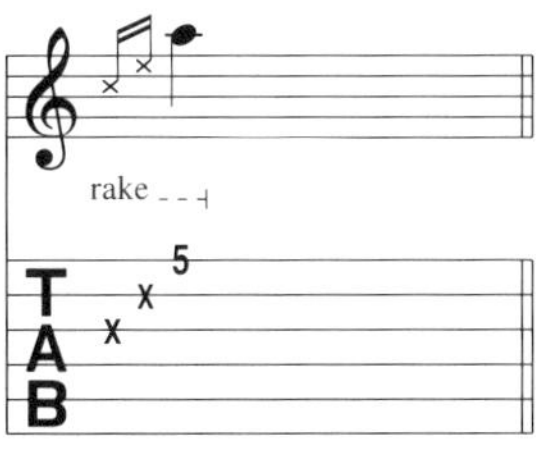

TREMOLO PICKING: The note is picked as rapidly and continuously as possible.

ARPEGGIATE: Play the notes of the chord indicated by quickly rolling them from bottom to top.

VIBRATO BAR DIVE AND RETURN: The pitch of the note or chord is dropped a specified number of steps (in rhythm) then returned to the original pitch.

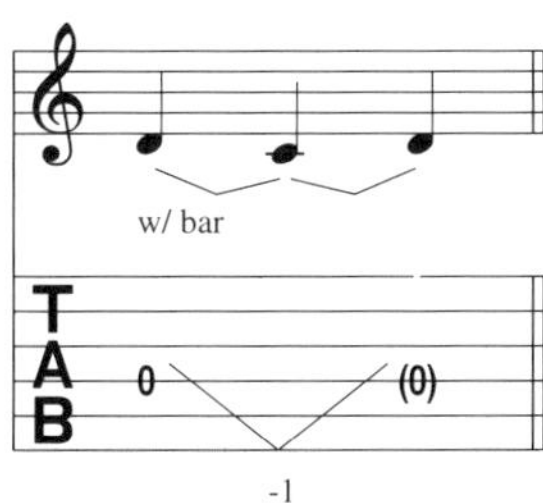

VIBRATO BAR SCOOP: Depress the bar just before striking the note, then quickly release the bar.

VIBRATO BAR DIP: Strike the note and then immediately drop a specified number of steps, then release back to the original pitch.

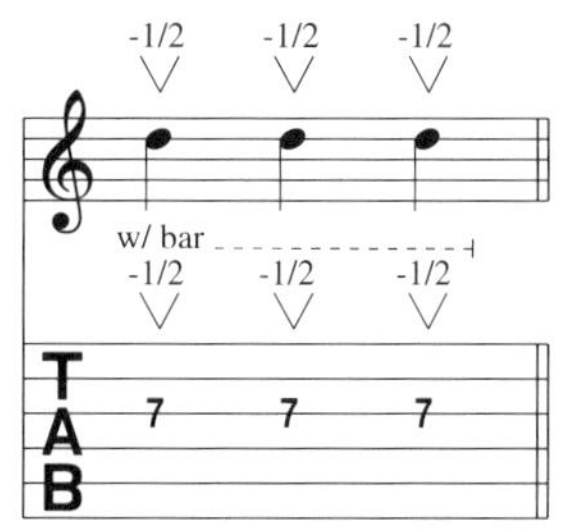

Additional Musical Definitions

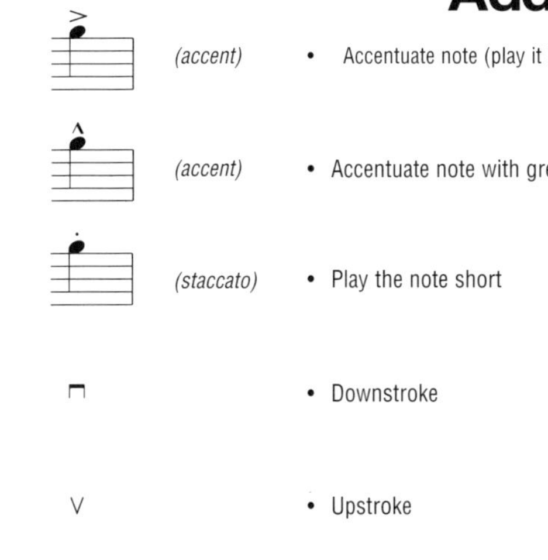

(accent) • Accentuate note (play it louder)

(accent) • Accentuate note with great intensity

(staccato) • Play the note short

• Downstroke

V • Upstroke

D.S. al Coda • Go back to the sign (𝄋), then play until the measure marked "***To Coda,***" then skip to the section labelled "***Coda.***"

D.S. al Fine • Go back to the beginning of the song and play until the measure marked "***Fine***" (end).

Rhy. Fig. • Label used to recall a recurring accompaniment pattern (usually chordal).

Riff • Label used to recall composed, melodic lines (usually single notes) which recur.

Fill • Label used to identify a brief melodic figure which is to be inserted into the arrangement.

Rhy. Fill • A chordal version of a Fill.

tacet • Instrument is silent (drops out).

• Repeat measures between signs.

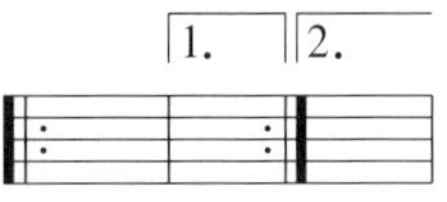

• When a repeated section has different endings, play the first ending only the first time and the second ending only the second time.

NOTE: Tablature numbers in parentheses mean:
1. The note is being sustained over a system (note in standard notation is tied), or
2. The note is sustained, but a new articulation (such as a hammer-on, pull-off, slide or vibrato begins, or
3. The note is a barely audible "ghost" note (note in standard notation is also in parentheses).

RECORDED VERSIONS

The Best Note-For-Note Transcriptions Available

RECORDED VERSIONS GUITAR

ALL BOOKS INCLUDE TABLATURE

No.	Title	Price
00690016	Will Ackerman Collection	$19.95
00690199	Aerosmith – Nine Lives	$19.95
00690146	Aerosmith – Toys in the Attic	$19.95
00694865	Alice In Chains – Dirt	$19.95
00694932	Allman Brothers Band – Volume 1	$24.95
00694933	Allman Brothers Band – Volume 2	$24.95
00694934	Allman Brothers Band – Volume 3	$24.95
00694877	Chet Atkins – Guitars For All Seasons	$19.95
00694918	Randy Bachman Collection	$22.95
00694880	Beatles – Abbey Road	$19.95
00694863	Beatles – Sgt. Pepper's Lonely Hearts Club Band	$19.95
00690383	Beatles – Yellow Submarine	$19.95
00690174	Beck – Mellow Gold	$17.95
00690346	Beck – Mutations	$19.95
00690175	Beck – Odelay	$17.95
00694884	The Best of George Benson	$19.95
00692385	Chuck Berry	$19.95
00692200	Black Sabbath – We Sold Our Soul For Rock 'N' Roll	$19.95
00690115	Blind Melon – Soup	$19.95
00690305	Blink 182 – Dude Ranch	$19.95
00690028	Blue Oyster Cult – Cult Classics	$19.95
00690219	Blur	$19.95
00694935	Boston: Double Shot Of	$22.95
00690237	Meredith Brooks – Blurring the Edges	$19.95
00690168	Roy Buchanon Collection	$19.95
00690364	Cake – Songbook	$19.95
00690337	Jerry Cantrell – Boggy Depot	$19.95
00690293	Best of Steven Curtis Chapman	$19.95
00690043	Cheap Trick – Best Of	$19.95
00690171	Chicago – Definitive Guitar Collection	$22.95
00690393	Eric Clapton – Selections from Blues	$19.95
00660139	Eric Clapton – Journeyman	$19.95
00694869	Eric Clapton – Live Acoustic	$19.95
00694896	John Mayall/Eric Clapton – Bluesbreakers	$19.95
00690162	Best of the Clash	$19.95
00690166	Albert Collins – The Alligator Years	$16.95
00694940	Counting Crows – August & Everything After	$19.95
00690197	Counting Crows – Recovering the Satellites	$19.95
00690118	Cranberries – The Best of	$19.95
00690215	Music of Robert Cray	$19.95
00694840	Cream – Disraeli Gears	$19.95
00690352	Creed – My Own Pirson	$19.95
00690007	Danzig 4	$19.95
00690184	dc Talk – Jesus Freak	$19.95
00690333	dc Talk – Supernatural	$19.95
00660186	Alex De Grassi Guitar Collection	$19.95
00690289	Best of Deep Purple	$17.95
00694831	Derek And The Dominos – Layla & Other Assorted Love Songs	$19.95
00690322	Ani Di Franco – Little Plastic Castle	$19.95
00690187	Dire Straits – Brothers In Arms	$19.95
00690191	Dire Straits – Money For Nothing	$24.95
00695382	The Very Best of Dire Straits – Sultans of Swing	$19.95
00660178	Willie Dixon – Master Blues Composer	$24.95
00690250	Best of Duane Eddy	$16.95
00690349	Eve 6	$19.95
00690323	Fastball – All the Pain Money Can Buy	$19.95
00690089	Foo Fighters	$19.95
00690235	Foo Fighters – The Colour and the Shape	$19.95
00690394	Foo Fighters – There Is Nothing Left to Lose	$19.95
00694920	Free – Best Of	$18.95
00690324	Fuel – Sunburn	$19.95
00690222	G3 Live – Satriani, Vai, Johnson	$22.95
00694807	Danny Gatton – 88 Elmira St	$19.95
00690127	Goo Goo Dolls – A Boy Named Goo	$19.95
00690338	Goo Goo Dolls – Dizzy Up the Girl	$19.95
00690117	John Gorka Collection	$19.95
00690114	Buddy Guy Collection Vol. A-J	$22.95
00690193	Buddy Guy Collection Vol. L-Y	$22.95
00694798	George Harrison Anthology	$19.95
00690068	Return Of The Hellecasters	$19.95
00692930	Jimi Hendrix – Are You Experienced?	$24.95
00692931	Jimi Hendrix – Axis: Bold As Love	$22.95
00692932	Jimi Hendrix – Electric Ladyland	$24.95
00690218	Jimi Hendrix – First Rays of the New Rising Sun	$24.95
00690038	Gary Hoey – Best Of	$19.95
00660029	Buddy Holly	$19.95
00660169	John Lee Hooker – A Blues Legend	$19.95
00690054	Hootie & The Blowfish – Cracked Rear View	$19.95
00694905	Howlin' Wolf	$19.95
00690136	Indigo Girls – 1200 Curfews	$22.95
00694938	Elmore James – Master Electric Slide Guitar	$19.95
00690167	Skip James Blues Guitar Collection	$16.95
00694833	Billy Joel For Guitar	$19.95
00694912	Eric Johnson – Ah Via Musicom	$19.95
00690169	Eric Johnson – Venus Isle	$22.95
00694799	Robert Johnson – At The Crossroads	$19.95
00693185	Judas Priest – Vintage Hits	$19.95
00690277	Best of Kansas	$19.95
00690073	B. B. King – 1950-1957	$24.95
00690098	B. B. King – 1958-1967	$24.95
00690134	Freddie King Collection	$17.95
00694903	The Best Of Kiss	$24.95
00690157	Kiss – Alive	$19.95
00690163	Mark Knopfler/Chet Atkins – Neck and Neck	$19.95
00690296	Patty Larkin Songbook	$17.95
00690070	Live – Throwing Copper	$19.95
00690018	Living Colour – Best Of	$19.95
00694845	Yngwie Malmsteen – Fire And Ice	$19.95
00694956	Bob Marley – Legend	$19.95
00690283	Best of Sarah McLachlan	$19.95
00690382	Sarah McLachlan – Mirrorball	$19.95
00690354	Sarah McLachlan – Surfacing	$19.95
00690239	Matchbox 20 – Yourself or Someone Like You	$19.95
00690244	Megadeath – Cryptic Writings	$19.95
00690236	Mighty Mighty Bosstones – Let's Face It	$19.95
00690040	Steve Miller Band Greatest Hits	$19.95
00694802	Gary Moore – Still Got The Blues	$19.95
00694958	Mountain, Best Of	$19.95
00694913	Nirvana – In Utero	$19.95
00694883	Nirvana – Nevermind	$19.95
00690026	Nirvana – Acoustic In New York	$19.95
00690121	Oasis – (What's The Story) Morning Glory	$19.95
00690290	Offspring, The – Ignition	$19.95
00690204	Offspring, The – Ixnay on the Hombre	$17.95
00690203	Offspring, The – Smash	$17.95
00694830	Ozzy Osbourne – No More Tears	$19.95
00694855	Pearl Jam – Ten	$19.95
00690053	Liz Phair – Whip Smart	$19.95
00690176	Phish – Billy Breathes	$22.95
00690331	Phish – The Story of Ghost	$19.95
00693800	Pink Floyd – Early Classics	$19.95
00694967	Police – Message In A Box Boxed Set	$70.00
00694974	Queen – A Night At The Opera	$19.95
00690395	Rage Against The Machine – The Battle of Los Angeles	$19.95
00690145	Rage Against The Machine – Evil Empire	$19.95
00690179	Rancid – And Out Come the Wolves	$22.95
00690055	Red Hot Chili Peppers – Bloodsugarsexmagik	$19.95
00690379	Red Hot Chili Peppers – Californication	$19.95
00690090	Red Hot Chili Peppers – One Hot Minute	$22.95
00694892	Guitar Style Of Jerry Reed	$19.95
00694937	Jimmy Reed – Master Bluesman	$19.95
00694899	R.E.M. – Automatic For The People	$19.95
00690260	Jimmie Rodgers Guitar Collection	$17.95
00690014	Rolling Stones – Exile On Main Street	$24.95
00690186	Rolling Stones – Rock & Roll Circus	$19.95
00690135	Otis Rush Collection	$19.95
00690031	Santana's Greatest Hits	$19.95
00694805	Scorpions – Crazy World	$19.95
00690150	Son Seals – Bad Axe Blues	$17.95
00690128	Seven Mary Three – American Standards	$19.95
00690076	Sex Pistols – Never Mind The Bollocks	$19.95
00120105	Kenny Wayne Shepherd – Ledbetter Heights	$19.95
00120123	Kenny Wayne Shepherd – Trouble Is	$19.95
00690196	Silverchair – Freak Show	$19.95
00690130	Silverchair – Frogstomp	$19.95
00690041	Smithereens – Best Of	$19.95
00694885	Spin Doctors – Pocket Full Of Kryptonite	$19.95
00690124	Sponge – Rotting Pinata	$19.95
00694921	Steppenwolf, The Best Of	$22.95
00694957	Rod Stewart – Acoustic Live	$22.95
00690021	Sting – Fields Of Gold	$19.95
00690242	Suede – Coming Up	$19.95
00694824	Best Of James Taylor	$16.95
00690238	Third Eye Blind	$19.95
00690267	311	$19.95
00690030	Toad The Wet Sprocket	$19.95
00690228	Tonic – Lemon Parade	$19.95
00690295	Tool – Aenima	$19.95
00699191	The Best of U2 – 1980-1990	$19.95
00694411	U2 – The Joshua Tree	$19.95
00690039	Steve Vai – Alien Love Secrets	$24.95
00690172	Steve Vai – Fire Garden	$24.95
00690023	Jimmie Vaughan – Strange Pleasures	$19.95
00690370	Stevie Ray Vaughan and Double Trouble – The Real Deal: Greatest Hits Volume 2	$22.95
00660136	Stevie Ray Vaughan – In Step	$19.95
00694835	Stevie Ray Vaughan – The Sky Is Crying	$19.95
00694776	Vaughan Brothers – Family Style	$19.95
00690217	Verve Pipe, The – Villains	$19.95
00120026	Joe Walsh – Look What I Did...	$24.95
00694789	Muddy Waters – Deep Blues	$24.95
00690071	Weezer	$19.95
00690286	Weezer – Pinkerton	$19.95
00694970	Who, The – Definitive Collection A-E	$24.95
00694971	Who, The – Definitive Collection F-Li	$24.95
00694972	Who, The – Definitive Collection Lo-R	$24.95
00694973	Who, The – Definitive Collection S-Y	$24.95
00690320	Best of Dar Williams	$17.95
00690319	Best of Stevie Wonder	$19.95
00690319	Stevie Wonder – Some of the Best	$19.95